Optimized Nutrition
A STRATEGIC GUIDE FOR
THE MARTIAL ARTIST.
Building big biceps
Volume 3
By:
Travis S. Miller,
(CISSN-NSCA-CSCS)

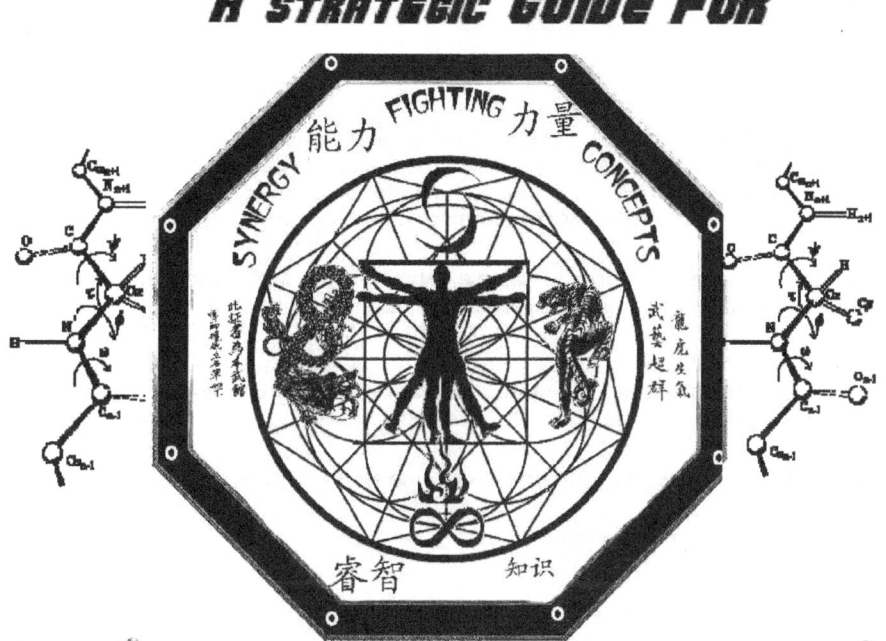

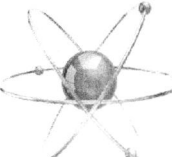

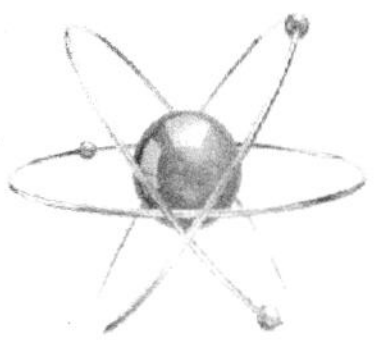

- Important Notice -

Before beginning any new exercise, nutrition or dietary supplement program you should consult a physician first. The information presented herein is not meant to treat or prevent any disease or to provide the reader with medical advice. If you are looking for specific medical advice then you should obtain this information from a licensed health-care practitioner.

This publication is intended for informational use only. Travis S. Miller and Optimized Nutrition will not assume any liability or be held responsible for

any form of injury, personal loss or illness caused by the utilization of this information. The individual results obtained from the use of this program will vary from person to person and we make no guarantee as to the degree of results that you will personally achieve.

This publication is fully copyrighted and does not come with giveaway or resale rights.

© 2014 - Travis S. Miller/Optimized Nutrition

- All Rights Reserved

Optimized Nutrition Volume, 3: building big biceps

Since the release of "Optimized Nutrition Vol. 1 and 2" I have received an over whelming response 10 times over asking for more info on nutrition/meal prep as well as training set. In this new volume 2 will focus on weight training sets/Reps and meal preps with recipes. And if it seems like I'm repeating on a subject that li have already covered once before GOOD!! FOR some reason I get a lot of same questions over again which they "The reader" should have read the book or chapters at least twice.

There is no way in hell that someone can read that much info at once and recall it step by step and thinks "No Man I got this" BULL SHIT!!! I suggest you read this book at least twice to obtain what you just read.

Travis's 'Idea' to building huge biceps stems from his combination of compound movements combined with regularly switching up exercises, which forces into a state of continuous adaptation. Getting trapped in routines leads to growth-killing plateaus. You don't have to worry about getting into a rut with the building big biceps program though because you'll never run out of routines and variations with everything he's included here.

With the foundation firmly established, Travis now gets into the actual training routines. The movements are organized into three categories: 1) mid-range power exercises; 2) fully stretched exercises; and 3) peaked contraction exercises. Squats, chins and dips are the first exercises he suggests for building big biceps. None of these are traditional bicep exercises but Travis says they're among the best movements you can do for the biceps.. These movements stress and stimulate the entire body, which means bigger gains everywhere.

In the remaining 100-plus pages Travis gets into the movements that make up the building big biceps program. I really like his detailed exercise descriptions and the fact that he also includes information about common mistakes to avoid throughout the book. The exercise descriptions are accompanied by photos showing the proper way to perform the movements. He also includes plenty of suggested routines for you to follow.

Overall, Travis lays out a winning program. building big biceps is not only thorough but realistic. It's not built on theory but his own personal experience as a Martial Artist and a strength coach. building big biceps is an easy read and the program is not difficult to follow. In my opinion, for building bigger biceps, Travis 's building big biceps program can't be beat.

Optimized Nutrition Volume, 3: **building big biceps**

Optimized Nutrition Volume, 3: building big biceps

Categories listings :

Introduction..........Page 1

Section 2:

Biceps..................Page 37

Section 3:

Triceps................Page 60

Section 4:

Forearms.............Page 74

Section 5:

Gaining Mass............Page 100

Section 6:

Supplement Stacking........Page 197

Section 7:

Rest and Recovery...........Page 218

Copyright © 2014 Travis S. Miller

All rights reserved

The Real Secret To Building Big Arms

How Would You Like To Add An Inch To Your Arms Over The Next Month?

Lets face it, everybody wants big, muscular arms.

You know the kind of arms I'm talking about, they sort of look full and square and usually have a garden hose sized vein running through them.

These are the kind of arms that command power and usually draw stares from everyone who sees them.

Yes, a big pair of arms is something that every weight trainer desperately wants.

It be nice to have a set of arms like that, wouldn't it? Well, if your reading this page, chances are, you'd like to have a pair of muscular arms.

How do you build big, muscular arms?

Now, I'm not going to lie to you. Only a lucky few will be able to attain 21 inch arms. Not all of us are genetically blessed to allow for that kind of arm growth. Don't feel bad because I got some great news for you. Anyone, can build big arms that are 18 or maybe even 19 inches round. Believe me, these are big arms and will be noticed no matter what your wearing.

Genetics aside, attaining big guns is possible for just about anyone and there is no real secret to building big arms. There are really two things you must remember when you are building big arms. First, big arms are not built by actually training arms. And second, if you want to build arms, you must prioritize their training.

Hold On! What Do You Mean Big Arms Are Not Built By Training Arms!

Alright, you got me. Your arms will grow if you train arms and prioritize them. What I'm talking about is to add some big poundage on certain movements that will allow for big time arm growth.

Let me ask you a question. What do you think will be more beneficial to your arm growth. Doing concentration curls with 20 pound dumbbells? Or doing a heavy set of bent over barbell rows using 225 pounds? How about doing triceps kick backs in comparison to heavy bench presses? I'll tell you right now with absolute certainty that barbell bent over rowing is going to be much more beneficial to your biceps growth than concentration curls. As will heavy bench presses will do for your triceps growth when compared to triceps kickbacks.

The real secret to building big arms are the compound movements. Compound movements are actually massive growth movements and must be performed if you ever want to get out of the 16 inch arm phase and move on to big time arms.

Believe me, no one has ever built big arms by simply doing triceps kickbacks and concentration curls. If you ever want to get a pair of 18 inch or 19 inch arms, you must perform heavy compound movements.

Optimized Nutrition Volume, 3: building big biceps

Compound movements are multi joint exercises that involve more than one muscle group. Compound movements allow you to use more weight than isolation exercises. I like to think of compound movements as "spreading the weight around" where each muscle involved has a chance to benefit from the weight being used.

For example, when you are doing a heavy bent over row, the actual target muscle group is the back but the biceps are almost directly involved. Now, if you were to perform the bent over row ala Dorian Yates style, you add even more biceps involvement. Since your body is naturally stronger in this movement, you will use heavier weight than if you were to do seated dumbbell curls.

What does this mean? Simply put, larger and stronger biceps.

The same can be said for the bench press. Although the targeted muscle group is the chest, the triceps and front deltoids are directly involved in the movement.

The point I'm trying to make is that you absolutely must stick to the heavy, compound movements if you ever want to have a pair of big arms. If your arms are under 16", drop all of the concentration curls and triceps kick backs type movements and go back to the basics. In fact, get rid of all isolation exercises in your training routine and go with compound movements. To this day, I don't do any isolation movements. Unless your dieting and preparing for a contest, get rid of them.

Examples of compound movements:

- Bench Press;
- Barbell Bent Over Rowing;
- Dead lifts;
- Standing Barbell Curls;
- Close Grip Bench Press;
- Shoulder Pressing;
- Chin Ups;
- Squats

The second secret to building big arms is prioritization. In order to improve anything, and that not only goes for body building or weight training, you need to give it your 100% attention and effort. If you want a big bench press, are you going to give it all your effort and attention? If you desperately want to make next year's football team, are you going to give this goal all of your effort and attention?

Arnold said it best. To improve a certain body part, you need to concentrate on that body part. I agree 100%. So, if you want to build a big pair of muscular arms, you have to train them first and give them 100% of your effort and attention.

On the first day of your training cycle, you will only train arms and nothing else. Keep all of your arm movements in the compounds range such as heavy close grip bench presses and heavy standing barbell curls.

Personally, if I want to improve a certain body part of get to a certain poundage in a movement, I'll train that particular body part with that particular exercise alone, with no other muscle group. For example, let's say I want to improve my calf development. This what I'll do. I'll train them first in my cycle and only train calves. By giving your muscle group priority and give it 100% of your attention and effort, they will have no other choice but to grow. This what you want to do for your arms.

I should also mention that you must consume an additional 500 calories per day. Simply drink another protein drink per day. If you want to grow, you must increase the amount of quality nutrients you are ingesting on a daily basis.

Try this drink as soon as your done your workout:

1 ½ cup strawberries
1 cup low fat strawberry yogurt
1 scoop(2oz) vanilla protein powder- 22 grams protein
1 tbsp honey
1 ½ cup low fat or 1% milk
1 cup orange juice
5 grams creatine monohydrate

Blend all ingredients in a blender until smooth.

Alright, now you have an idea of what is involved in building a big pair of arms. I'm going to give you an arm workout that prioritizes arms and uses compound movements for big time growth. You can find the complete workout at:

Lesson 1 -
"A Lesson You MUST Learn In Order To Build Big Muscular Arms"

When I first started out weight training, I was motivated and ambitious. I remember seeing a picture of Lance Dreher (80's body builder) and was simply mesmerized by the size and shape of his arms. His arms had this square look to them, that seemed to take on a life of their own, with a garden sized hose sized vein running right through them. His arms exuded power and beauty at the same time.

After reading all the popular muscle building books, such as MuslceMag and Muscle and Fitness, I dove right in and started doing the routines of the body building pro's. I hit the weights, hard and heavy, doing the Arnold workouts from start to finish. I took my 120 pound body to it's limits, and more, each and every workout.

After a couple of months of this, I noticed that I wasn't making any progress whatsoever. My arms didn't look anywhere near Lance's. My pythons stretched the tape to just over 14 inches.

Why?

Looking back, I can see now that I was a complete noob with no idea or understanding of progression, technique, or nutrition. I started doing 20 to 25 sets per body part and trying to go hard and heavy on each of those sets. Right off the bat, I went heavy doing 2 to 3 repetitions, just like the pro's. I wanted to jump to the advanced level without paying my dues.

You see, besides not being a drugged up pro body builder, I was a total beginner with no inner body awareness or understanding of progression. Progression being the dominant word here.

You see, progression is defined as "forward or onward movement" in the dictionary and correctly sums up the entire muscle building process. That is, in order to make progression, there needs to be a beginning.

Optimized Nutrition Volume, 3: building big biceps

Proper progression starts with a beginning.

My problem was that I didn't give my body and brain a proper place to start in order to have a progression plan in place. I jumped to a pro body building routine right from the start when I should have started at a place where my body could make proper muscle growth progression.

This is one of the most important lessons I can give anyone trying to build muscle mass.

You must have a starting point. This means starting out slowly and using weights that provide your brain and body with a starting foundation. How are you supposed to build a house when you don't know where to start? It's like trying to put up the sides of a house with no foundation. What do you think's going to happen?

The same goes for your body.

Building muscle is a progression of short, physical improvements - That's it. You need to have a starting point and build upon that starting point in order to make these improvements. After each cycle of improvements, you take a short rest and you start the process all over, but at this time, at a higher level than your previous start.

I've been in this game for over 20 years and if there is one lesson that I think you must understand, it's this concept. Once you understand this principle, everything will fall into place. With that in mind, I've structured the big arm routine on this principle. After reading the big arm guide, you will notice that your not making the jump to super heavy weights right off the bat. You may even think it looks quite easy and straight forward.

Bingo! This is what building muscle is all about. Start slow and progress to higher and higher levels of intensity until your workouts are taking your body to levels you never thought possible. You do this in "weight training cycles" and over time, you will notice your muscles getting, bigger, bigger, and bigger.

This is how it's done and something I am showing you in the big arms guide. Please, don't let anyone tell you different. Building muscle (and big arms) is all about progression.

Four Weeks To Larger Arms!

That's right, how would you like to kick start your arm training program that will start adding new size to your arms in as little as 4 weeks?

I thought you might be interested...

Training arms is fun. Really, it's just so much fun training arms, knowing that with each passing workout they get bigger and bigger.

Unlike legs, which can be brutally hard (Which explains all the big arms and little legs out there), training arms is fun, exciting, and requires little work (relative to big muscle groups such as the back and legs).

Optimized Nutrition Volume, 3: building big biceps

Sometimes, I just get the urge to add a little more size to my arms and just train the hell out of them. I'll usually get this way just before summer when I know my arms are going to hanging out of a t-shirt.

I get a ton of questions about how to build big arms so, I thought, why not put together a quick and dirty arm training program. So, for this month's workout, I thought I'd pass on a 4 week arm routine.

Alright, lets get into it.

The first thing I have to say about building big arms is that they need to be given priority over everything else. What you want to do is train them first in your weight lifting cycle and you'll only train arms and nothing else. This way, you give them 100 percent of your effort and attention. Rest assured that once you start to do this, your arms will start to grow (assuming your diet is in place).

What were going to do is break up the routine into sections. There are 6 sections that you will follow for this particular arm routine. They are:

- Prioritization
- Exercise Routine
- Diet
- Supplementation
- Water
- Rest

So let's get into it.

Prioritization

The first and most important thing that you must do with any body part is to prioritize that area. What you will do is train this body part first and foremost. So, we want to build bigger arms so the best thing to do is start our training cycle with arms.

This is very important. Because we want to build a huge set of arms, we will only train arms on the start of our training cycle and nothing else. That means you won't train chest, back or any other body part with arms.

Exercise Routine

Your training routine is going to be very specialized so be prepared to put in the work that's need in order to grow some huge arms. The first thing to do is take a look at your current training program and get rid of the stuff you don't need. Get rid of any exercise with cables. If you have cable cross overs or anything like that, get rid of them.

What were going to do here is prime your body for growth. To do this, we need to do some heavy, compound lifting. You don't grow using cables and machines. You get big muscles by using heavy compound exercises. Don't let anyone tell you different because there is absolutely no question about this one.

Optimized Nutrition Volume, 3: building big biceps

The next thing you want to do is incorporate muscle building exercises into your program. This means adding the following exercises to your routine:

Chest:

• Bench Press (barbell or dumbbells)
• Incline Press (barbell or dumbbells)
• Dips

Back:

• Bent Over Barbell Rows
• Deadlifts
• Close Grip Pull downs

Shoulders:

• Seated Press (barbells or dumbbells)

Legs:

• Squats
• Leg Press

Biceps:

• Barbell Curls
• Dumbbell Curls

Triceps:

• Close Grip Bench Press
• Lying Triceps Extensions

Abs:

• Incline sit ups

Calves:

• Standing Calf Raises

It is very important that you get these exercises into your routine and drop all cable movements or other exercises that have no direct impact on growth. Here is the goal of your new weight training routine: To train each body part, hard and heavy with core compound movements while getting the optimal rest in order to grow like a madman. Remember this and you will grow beyond your wildest dreams.

Here is a sample routine:

<u>Day one</u>
Biceps, Triceps and abs

<u>Day two</u>
Quadriceps, hamstrings, and calves

<u>Day three</u>
Rest

<u>Day four</u>
Chest and abs

<u>Day five</u>
Rest

<u>Day six</u>
Shoulders and back

<u>Day seven</u>
Rest

Repeat

The Arm Routine

The arm routine you are going to follow is two fold. The first thing is your going to pump your arms with blood using compound movements. The second thing is to alternate certain exercises. Here is the routine:

Biceps, Triceps, and Abs

<u>Biceps super set with triceps</u>

Exercise 1:

Standing barbell curls super set with close grip bench presses;

Warm up 1 x 20 reps
First set: 1 x 12 reps
Second set: 1 x 10 reps
Third set: 1 x 7 reps
Fourth set: 1 x 7 reps

Exercise 2:

Seated alternate dumbbell curls super set with standing triceps extensions;

First set: 1 x 12 reps
Second set: 1 x 10 reps
Third set: 1 x 7 reps
Fourth set: 1 x 7 reps

Exercise 3:

Preacher curls super set with lying triceps extensions;

First set: 1 x 10 reps
Second set: 1 x 8 reps
Third set: 1 x 8 reps
Fourth set: 1 x 12 reps

Abs

Crunches

4 x 20 reps

For those of you who don't know what a super set is, it's this:

Train two opposing muscle groups with little rest in between each exercise.

An example of super setting is alternating biceps curls with triceps push-down with minimum rest between exercises. So, you would first do a set of biceps curls and then head over to do a set of triceps push-down with little or no rest in between this period. That's one super set.

What's the use of a super set? Let me give you a quick story. Back in my body building days, I was training in Toronto, Canada and one of the guys I used to compete against starting training at our local gym. I remember this guy because he was huge! His arms in particular were an awesome sight. Anyways, he started training at our gym and I noticed something very peculiar in the way he trained his arms.

He super setted all of his upper arm movements. At the time, I couldn't understand it. I mean, he didn't use super heavy weight for his movements. He used moderate weight and practised control on all of his exercises. Anyways, I asked him why he trained his arms this way and he said it made his arms feel like they were about to explode. This method pumped his arms up to super size like no other program did. So, I decided to try it out and to this day, this is my main arm workout. That was 15 years ago!

Optimized Nutrition Volume, 3: building big biceps

I use this routine on all of my arm workouts and have been using it for a long time. I don't change the workout because it works for me every time. The workout will pump your arms up like they've never been pumped before.

The second thing your going to do is alternate the first biceps exercise. That is, for the first two weeks, your going to do heavy barbell curls for your first exercise and than for following two weeks, your going to do alternate dumbbell curls first and barbell curls as your second exercise. Here it is:

Weeks 1 and 2:

Biceps, Triceps, and Abs

Biceps super set with triceps

Exercise 1:

Standing barbell curls super set with close grip bench presses;

Warm up 1 x 20 reps
First set: 1 x 12 reps
Second set: 1 x 10 reps
Third set: 1 x 7 reps
Fourth set: 1 x 7 reps

Exercise 2:

Seated alternate dumbbell curls super set with standing triceps extensions;

First set: 1 x 12 reps
Second set: 1 x 10 reps
Third set: 1 x 7 reps
Fourth set: 1 x 7 reps

Exercise 3:

Preacher curls super set with Lying triceps extensions;

First set: 1 x 10 reps
Second set: 1 x 8 reps
Third set: 1 x 8 reps
Fourth set: 1 x 12 reps

Abs

Crunches

4 x 20 reps

Weeks 3 and 4:

Biceps super set with triceps

Exercise 1:

Seated alternate dumbbell curls super set with close grip bench presses;

Warm up 1 x 20 reps
First set: 1 x 12 reps
Second set: 1 x 10 reps
Third set: 1 x 7 reps
Fourth set: 1 x 7 reps

Exercise 2:

Standing barbell curls super set with standing triceps extensions;

First set: 1 x 12 reps
Second set: 1 x 10 reps
Third set: 1 x 7 reps
Fourth set: 1 x 7 reps

Exercise 3:

Preacher curls super set with Lying triceps extensions;

First set: 1 x 10 reps
Second set: 1 x 8 reps
Third set: 1 x 8 reps
Fourth set: 1 x 12 reps

Abs

Crunches

4 x 20 reps

As you can see, we've alternated standing barbell curls with seated dumbbell curls for the last 2 weeks.

This will be your arm routine for the first 4 weeks.

Diet

I'm going to be honest with you. If your dieting to lose weight and burn fat, your not going to get the results your looking for with this type of routine. If you want to grow and build muscle, your going to have to feed your body every two hours with nutrient dense foods. If you can't commit to eating every two hours or so, than this routine won't work for you.

Supplementation

I'm not going to say that you absolutely must use supplements if you want to grow because you don't. What I will say is this. Supplements have a way of adding a new dimension to your training provided you have a well balanced diet in place. If you don't have a good diet in place, than supplements are a waste of time and money.

However, if you do have a sound diet in place, supplements can greatly enhance your weight training program. However, you have to make sure you choose supplements that actually work.

Prior to each meal, I take 4 liver tabs. I've been doing this for years and all I can say is that these little things will work like magic if you follow a sound diet.

Water

Personally, water is underestimated when it comes to building muscle. Sure, we hear all about how you need a lot of water to help you lose weight, but what about building muscle? Why is it so important? Muscle rely on water for muscle contraction. If your dehydrated, your muscles won't be at their best. I'm not going to get into this right here but if you want (and should!) know the importance of water. to find out the importance of water and building muscle.

Rest

You need a lot of rest if you want to grow. I'm going to assume that you know the benefits of rest so try and get at least 8 hours of sleep each night. For the next 4 weeks, stay out of the bars and cut back on all the booze. One night out and your whole schedule is ruined so try and stay away from the bars and parties.

Alright, so there you have it. If you're committed to building an impressive set of arms, you have at your finger tips the knowledge of how to do it. So it is now up to you.

A Dumbbell Workout For The Upper Arms

Optimized Nutrition Volume, 3: building big biceps

Let me tell you straight, there's nothing wrong with using dumbbells to build your arms.

Using dumbbells is a great way to workout. You don't need to go to a gym, you don't need a whole lot of space, you really don't need any fancy equipment, and you can use dumbbells anywhere in the house.

I personally love to train with dumbbells and I strongly believe that they can offer benefits that you that you simply can't get with a barbell.

For example, since dumbbell forces muscle groups to work independently of one another, you can work your right and left side muscle groups evenly. Have you ever noticed how one arm is always stronger than the other? If you answered yes to this question, your going to have to start using dumbbells in your training routine.

I vividly remember how my left arm was always stronger than the right. Since I primarily used barbells and machines, (at that time) for most of my exercises, my left arm got most of the benefit. The balance is set up on the barbells and machines in favour of your stronger muscle groups. This in turn, throws you muscle balance off because your stronger body part will most always grow bigger than it's weaker counterpart.

Anyways, after some guidance, I started all my workouts with dumbbells. After about three months, my right arm caught up with my left. In fact, today, my right arm is a little stronger than my left. I'll tell you this though, dumbbells don't lie and 50 pounds is 50 pounds. With barbells and machines, you can get away with moving a certain amount of weight because your stronger muscle group compensates for the weaker muscle group. With dumbbells, you can't do that. Each side has to pull it's own weight, so to speak.

Another great thing about working out with dumbbells is the fact that they provide a different plane of motion than barbells. Take the seated dumbbell curl for example. With a barbell, the weight comes up and goes down. However, with a slight twist of the wrist, you can greatly enhance the exercise using dumbbells. Take a look at this page here:

With that in mind, I want to pass on a dumbbell arm workout that will help strengthen and build your arms. You will train biceps first, and than train the triceps. The biceps routine has three exercises while the triceps routine has 2. I suggest performing this dumbbell arm workout routine once per week, twice at the most.

Also, I suggest you start the workout with a 5 minute, light aerobic exercise such as the elliptical trainer, treadmill, or exercise bike. If you don't have any aerobic equipment, try running on the spot for 3 to 5 minutes. It is very important to the blood flowing throughout the body before exercising.

Let' take a look at the exercises for the dumbbell arm routine:

Biceps Exercises:

1) The Standing Dumbbell Curl;
2) The Incline Dumbbell Curl;
3) The Concentration Curl

Optimized Nutrition Volume, 3: building big biceps

Triceps Exercises:

1) Seated Single Dumbbell Extensions;
2) The Triceps Kick Back

The Workout

Biceps

Exercise #1 - The Standing Dumbbell Curl

Warm up: 1 x 15 repetitions
3 sets of 10 repetitions

Exercise #2 - The Incline Dumbbell Curl

3 sets of 10 repetitions

Exercise #3 - The Dumbbell Concentration Curl

2 sets of 12 repetitions

Triceps

Exercise #4 - Seated Single Dumbbell Extensions

Optimized Nutrition Volume, 3: building big biceps

Warm up: 1 x 15 repetitions
3 sets of 12 repetitions

Exercise #5 - The Triceps Kick Back

3 sets of 12 repetitions

This is a pretty simple dumbbell routine but it will work if you remember to be consistent and to constantly try and improve. Remember, buying more weight because your getting stronger is a good thing. This means your arms are growing so don't worry if you have to go out and get more weight.

I'd like to pass on some valuable tips for you to use in combination with the arm routine. Follow the weight training advice on this page and you'll start gaining quality muscle mass.

There you have it, a simple dumbbell arm workout routine that you can perform at the gym or at home. It's a very basic dumbbell routine but an effective one. If you feel that the weight is getting light, you might want to add some more weight to the dumbbell.

I'm Going To Show You How You Can Add Inches To Your Biceps!"

Today, I'd like to provide you with some much needed information about how to get big biceps.

Now, I'm sure if your reading this page, your looking to add some size to your biceps.

I'm sure that you've also done some initial research on the internet looking for some guidance about programs and techniques.

I've also done some research on how to get big biceps and there is some conflicting information about what programs to follow, what exercises to do and so forth.

Optimized Nutrition Volume, 3: building big biceps

With that in mind, I'm going to give you, what I think are the best techniques to building big biceps.

The way I look at it, is if you want to get big biceps, your going to have to train them in a very specific way that is conducive to building muscle. I've broken down the main steps and they are as follows:

1) Know Where Your Going
2) Specialization
3) Exercise Periods
4) Exercise Selection - Direct Exercises
5) Exercise Selection - Indirect Exercises
6) Muscle Building Exercises
7) Diet
8) Rest
9) Supplements

What I'd like to do is go over each and discuss the important of each in terms of how to get big biceps.

1) Know Where Your Going

Simply showing up to the gym and doing 10 sets of barbell curls will do nothing for your biceps growth. The first thing you need to do is get a starting point. The only way to do this is take out a measuring tape and weight scale.

And save this log to your desktop. Once you've done this, print it out. Write down your measurements in this log. The next thing your going to do is hop on a weight scale and take down your weight. Write this number down in the log. Remember, date the log.

What you're doing here is getting a starting point, which is very, very important in weight training. Once you know what your starting point is, you can decide what your goals are. Realistically, you can probably expect to gain anywhere from ½ " to 1 ½ " to your biceps in a 12 week training cycle. That is, of course if you do everything right.

So, if your arms are 15", you can realistically expect an increase to 15 ½ inches to 16 ½ inches. This all depends on how dedicated you are with your training and diet. Setting a goal for 20 inch arms is unrealistic. Only a small percentage of the population can attain a 20 inch arm. Of course, this all depends on your genetics and this will determine how big your biceps can get - Over a period of time (usually years). However, 18" and 19" arms are realistic (Over the course of a few years) and believe me, these are pretty big arms.

Take small steps in terms of periodic training cycles, and you'll reach your goals. Ok, write down your goal and in 12 weeks your going to see that you've reached this measurement.

Now, your going to be taking your arm measurements every week as well as your body weight. Each should be increasing with each measurement.

Alright, now that you know where your starting, you can get onto attaining your goals.

2) Specialization

This probably the most important aspect to improving any body part. However, it's one that is not really discussed in the muscle magazines or the internet. I first heard about specialization when I was reading an interview article with the great Arnold. He said that whenever he wanted to improve a body part, he would make it a priority in his weight training program. It only makes sense that if you want to improve something, you step up your efforts to make sure it improves.

Take calves for example. Most people with weak calves will say that they simply don't have the genetics for building huge calves. However, if you take a look at their training routines, you'll see calves tucked deep down after training quadriceps, and hamstrings, doing maybe 3 to 4 sets of light calf raises. It doesn't work like that. I order to improve a weak body part, you have to train it like it's your favorite body part.

I hope you understand that to truly build big biceps, you need to specialize and train them first and foremost. Here's what I suggest. Train your biceps and triceps on the first day of you training program. You will have to re-structure your current weight training program but believe me, if you want big biceps, your going to have to. Here's a sample training schedule:

<u>Day 1</u>
Biceps and Triceps

<u>Day 2</u>
Legs

<u>Day 3</u>
Rest

<u>Day 4</u>
Back and Chest

<u>Day 5</u>
Rest

<u>Day 6</u>
Shoulders

<u>Day 7</u>
Rest

This is just a sample and you will have to come up with a weight training plan that is suitable for you.

Alright, now that you know that specialization is needed to build big biceps, let's move on to the third point.

3) Exercise Periods

The thing you have to remember about biceps is that they are a small muscle group. It doesn't take much work in order to stimulate growth but there is a very fine line when it comes to doing too much for the biceps.

Biceps overtraining is a common thing and what people fail to understand is that any pulling motion involves the biceps. This is probably one of the main reasons why hard working weight trainers can't seem to get their biceps to grow.

Your biceps are constantly being worked from other exercises and really, they only need brief, intense workout sessions to cause growth. For this reason, I would say to train them once per week. Yep, only once per week. Trust me, if your doing everything right, once per week is all you need and you will see the results your looking for.

When you structure your training program, just make sure that you give your biceps enough rest periods to cause muscle growth. Training back a day after you've trained biceps is not a smart thing to do. If you're doing it now, stop immediately. What you want to do is give your biceps at least two to three days rest in between each training session. See the above sample weight training routine.

I'm going to tell you right now, that compound movements such as barbell bent over rows, and chin ups provide just as much muscle stimulation, if not more, than regular biceps exercises. I'm going to discuss this shortly but just remember, indirect exercises are the main biceps builders in your training program.

Alright, now that you know about exercise timing, lets move onto the next point about how to get big biceps.

4) Exercise Selection - Direct Exercises

I'm going to tell you right now that you don't need 25 sets for biceps. Doing 5 exercises for 5 sets is not a smart way to train. Drop the Arnold workouts and cut down on the amount of sets and exercises your doing for biceps.

Really, your only need 3 exercises for the biceps and that's plenty. Here is a sample biceps workout to do:

Biceps Exercise #1 - <u>Standing Barbell Curls</u>

Warm up: 1 x 20 repetitions
Set one: 1 x 8 repetitions with 50% of your maximum
Set two: 1 x 8 repetitions with 60% of your maximum
Set three: 1 x 8 repetitions with 70% of your maximum
Set four: 1 x 8 repetitions with 80% of your maximum

Biceps Exercise #2 - Seated Dumbbell Curls

Set one: 1 x 10 repetitions with 60% of your maximum
Set two: 1 x 10 repetitions with 70% of your maximum
Set three: 1 x 8 repetitions with 80% of your maximum
Set four: 1 x 8 repetitions with 80% of your maximum

Biceps Exercise #3 - Preacher Curls

4 sets of 12 repetitions

For preacher curls you should be using moderate weight for this exercise since you really want to do this exercise nice and slow.

This is all you need to really stimulate your biceps. Anymore is overkill and you might be doing more harm than good. Remember, less is more!

Here's a very important point that I'd like to make. With each workout, you must improve. You can either use more weight, more reps, or do the workout faster. If you don't improve from workout to workout, there is no reason why your body needs to grow. You see, improvement means growth. Understand this principle and you'll build huge muscles.

Now that you have an idea of what you should be doing for your biceps workouts, let's move on to the next point about how to get big biceps.

5) Exercise Selection - Indirect Exercises

Alright, this is very important so you may want to listen up. You absolutely must have compound pulling movements in your weight training program. If you want to build big biceps, your going to have to start doing these exercises. What I'm talking about are bent over barbell rowing, T bar rows, seated pulley's, single arm dumbbell rows, dead lifts and chin ups. What you want to do is incorporate these exercises into your back routine and not your biceps routine.

Let's take the above noted sample training schedule. On day 4, you will train back and shoulders. I want you to train back first and really concentrate on moving some heavy weight. The majority of your back exercises should be compound movements.

Whenever I need to add some size to my arms, I add in core compound movements. Believe me, your biceps will receive much more muscle stimulation doing a heavy set of reverse grip barbell bent rows than they will with concentration curls.

Here's a sample back routine that includes compound movements:

Exercise # 1 - Chin Ups
3 x 12 repetitions

Exercise # 2 - Reverse Grip Barbell Bent Over Row
4 x 8 repetitions

Exercise # 3 - Seated Cable Pulley Rows
3 x 10 repetitions

Exercise # 4 - Standing Dumbbell Shrugs
4 x 12 repetitions

Nothing fancy about this back routine but it is very effective for building a big back and especially effective for building big biceps.

Now, you should be spacing your back workout about 3 days apart from doing your main biceps workout. See the above noted sample workout routine.

Ok, now that you know the importance of core, back movements, let's move onto the next point about building big biceps.

6) Muscle Building Exercises

These exercise are not directly involved in your biceps routine but they are pure muscle builders. The two main exercise you may want to incorporate into your training routine are squats and dead lifts. Your probably thinking, what does squats have to do with biceps training? Well, everything. Doing heavy squats has a magical way of making your whole body grow. The reason is that they require so much effort and intensity to do them that it causes a huge surge of growth hormone and testosterone release in your body. As you may or may not know, these hormones are responsible for muscle growth. The more natural production of these hormones you have in your body, the better.

So remember, do your squats in your leg sessions.

Lets move onto the next point about how to get big biceps.

7) Diet

In order to get big strong arms, you need to build muscle mass. In order to build large muscles, you need to increase your intake of nutrients. If you're thinking that you can add two inches of muscle to your arms while trying to get a six pack of abs, it's not going to happen. Building muscle mass required calories, and lots of them. Drop the six pack abs diet and get on a diet that's loaded with plenty of calories, protein, carbs, and quality fats.

I'll be very honest here, you want to actually add body weight here in order to start building big biceps. If you want to get big and strong, you have to start eating to get big.

Ok, now that you understand that you need to gain lean body weight to build big biceps, lets move onto our next point.

8) Rest

I'll keep this nice and simple. Get at least 8 hours of sleep each and every night. Late nights and parties will kill your progress and should be avoided at all costs if you want to build big biceps.

It is very important that you get into the habit of getting quality rest every night. What you have to remember is that your body actually grows and builds muscle while you are sleeping, not while your weight training. If you can get the necessary <u>rest</u>, your body will use that time to repair and build muscle tissue, which is what you want.

9) Supplements

Supplements have there place in sports and weight training. However, the most important point to remember about supplements is that they only work once your have your diet and training in place. Supplements help to enhance a weight training program that's already working. I'd only suggest that you use supplements after 6 to 8 weeks of steady weight training. This way, your body will make the most of these sports supplements. If you feel you are ready to use supplements and are interested in using them to help with your weight training program,

Alright, there you have it, a formula that shows you how to get big biceps. If you can implement the above mentioned points, I'm sure you'll build the kind of biceps your looking for.

The One Day Arm Blasting Routine

What if I was to tell you that you that it is possible for you to increase your arm size in one day? How about a half an inch? Maybe an inch?

Yep, it is possible and believe it or not, there is a way to add some serious size to your upper arms. And all within 24 hours.

I remember my buddy at the gym telling me about this routine when I was in my early 20's.

I didn't believe a word he was telling me but one day, I decided to try the routine out.

We took about 4 days to prepare and we hit the gym on a Saturday. I have to admit, the workout was hard. But the results, were quite amazing to say the least.

Now, this workout is not for everyone and can only be performed once every two or three months. This is a tough workout that will leave your arms with a throbbing, muscular pump for the better part of a week. Therefore, it should only be attempted by serious weight trainers. Your training, eating, and supplementation has to be at optimal levels before you attempt this program.

Optimized Nutrition Volume, 3: building big biceps

So, if your serious about adding some size to your arms, please read on. Remember, this program is for one day only but you will be spending the better part of the day in the gym. If your not prepared to do this, you should not attempt the program.

What you need to do before attempting the arm blitz program:

In order to prepare yourself for this program, your going to have to follow some rules.

First rule: Do not train for at least 4 days prior to attempting this program. Yup, 4 whole days of doing nothing - Just resting. This program works best if your body is fully rested and primed to blast your arms.

Second rule: Concentrate on eating massive amounts of food. You will need to gather all of your resources in order to get the greatest benefit from this type of program. I'm sure you are aware that in order to build the optimal amount of muscle, you have to ensure that your body gets the optimal amount of food - Well, it goes double for this program.

One week prior to using the one day arm blasting routine, you will need to go on an eating binge. No, I don't mean going to your nearest MacDonald's and stuffing yourself with quarter pounders. I'm talking about clean, muscle building food. Here's what you can do - Schedule a "get big" day, usually one day ahead of the arm routine..

Protein intake should be no less than 1.5 to 2.0 grams. Remember, you want to pump your body with top grade fuel. That means quality carbohydrates. You diet should be at in between 50% and 65% of high quality carbohydrates. Your going to need plenty of stored glycogen in your muscles for this program.

This fuel is vital if you ware to endure the assault on your arms. Plenty of pasta, rice, potatoes, breads, and other supplements are required for this carbohydrate loading phase.

Also, remember to consume quality fats such as flax and canola oil. Simply add a teaspoon to your protein shakes two times per day and this should do the trick. Fats are very important for hard working weight trainers so don't neglect them.

Eat 6 to 8 nutritious meals every day to take in the necessary amount of protein and carbs.

I know, this may seem like a lot but it is needed. Now in order to help you with the large protein intake, you can use supplements to help you.

Supplementation:

You don't have to take in supplements but I strongly suggest it. I suggest you take a quality vitamin/mineral supplement as soon as you finish your breakfast. Also, I suggest you use a quality protein powder such as Dymatize's Mega Milk or optimum nutrition's whey powder and a quality creatine product.

I strongly suggest you use something like Dymatize Xpand or San V 12. I don't know what it is but these creatine supplements do wonders, much more so than regular creatine.

You should be consuming at least 2 to 3 servings of protein powder per day along with 2 servings of creatine. I suggest consuming the protein powder in between meals - at least 30 to 40 grams of protein per serving. As for the creatine, try consuming a serving as soon as you wake up and in the afternoon, preferably on an empty stomach or near empty stomach.

Optimized Nutrition Volume, 3: building big biceps

Bear in mind that you should not skip meals (very important!), so your late afternoon creatine cocktail, can be no longer that three hours after eating. So if you eat lunch at 12:30 pm, have a serving of creatine no later than 3:00 pm.

For my protein shakes, I've been using Dymatize's "Mega Milk" for the past two months and I've been very pleased with the results. I have no problem recommending this protein drink.

You should also be taking in lots and lots of water. The last thing you want to do is go in to the gym dehydrated. You won't make any gains if your body is in need of water. I suggest you take in at least 10 glasses of water per day. Take two as soon as you get up.

Also, make sure you get plenty of sleep time. Try to get at least 8 hours of sleep per night.

Now, your going to have to bring a about 4 protein drinks with you as well as a creatine drink with you. The protein drinks will need to be mixed with water or skim milk and a banana mixed in. I suggest you bring your drinks in two large containers (for the protein drink) and one for the creatine drink. Try and store them in cool place.

Alright, let's get on with the workout. Here's what your going to do.

6:00 am:

Wake up and have two glasses of water. Take in one serving of creatine.

7:00 am:

Have one cup of oatmeal with a bit of brown sugar and raisins. Have a protein drink and one apple. Follow this up with a vitamin and mineral tablet or pack.

7:30 am:

Arrive at the gym and take your pre workout measurements. Hope on the exercise bike for 5 minutes and get yourself going. Stretch out a bit and do a light set of barbell curls and triceps push downs. Remember, you want to warm the muscle up.

8:00 am: Workout #1

Grab a barbell and load it with enough weight that you can do 10 good reps. Now only do 8 reps with it. The reps should be clean with no cheating. Nice and smooth and make sure that you don't take it to failure. Your in for a long day so pace yourself.

Now, do the same for triceps. Pick a weight that you can do 10 good reps with on the standing triceps push down apparatus and do only 8. As the same with barbell curls, this exercise should be done in strict form. That's one superset.

There is no rest between exercises, but allow yourself 35 seconds rest between supersets. Complete 3 more sets in the same fashion. Remember, keep the weight constant. This workout should take you about 5 minutes or so. After your done, take a breather until 8:30 am. Remember to drink water as you workout.

8:30 am: Workout #2

Grab a set of dumbbells that will challenge you for 12 quality reps of seated alternate curls. Now, only perform 10 reps and not 12. Upon completion, immediately go to lying french presses (skull crushers), and pick a weight that you can do 12 quality reps with. However, only do 10 reps in super strict form. Rest for about 35 seconds and repeat this superset for 3 more sets.

This should take you 5 minutes or so to complete. Take a breather until 9:00 am.

9:00 am: Repeat Workout #1

9:30 am: Repeat Workout #2

10:00 am: Repeat Workout #1

10:30 am: Repeat Workout #2

11:00 am: Repeat Workout #1

11:30 am: Repeat Workout #2

11:45 am: Have a protein drink with water or skim milk and one banana blended in.

12:00 noon: Repeat Workout #1

12:30 pm: Repeat Workout #2

12:45 pm: Have a serving of creatine.

1:00 pm: Repeat Workout #1

1:30 pm: Repeat Workout #2

1:45 pm: Have a protein drink with water or skim milk and one banana blended in.

2:00 pm: Repeat Workout #1

2:30 pm: Repeat Workout #2

3:00 pm: Repeat Workout #1

3:30 pm: Repeat Workout #2

3:45 pm: Have a protein drink with water or skim milk and one banana blended in.

4:00 pm: Repeat Workout #1

4:30 pm: Repeat Workout #2

4:45 pm: Have a protein drink with water or skim milk and one banana blended in. At this time, you are finished your workout and should be on your way home.

5:45 pm: Have one serving of creatine.

6:30 pm: Eat a large meal consisting if chicken, rice, and vegetables. You can also have steak, rice and veggies.

7:45 pm: 1 cup of cottage cheese with 8 almonds tossed in with 1/2 can of mandarin slices addin. Have this with one whole wheat bagel, toasted with 1 tbsp of peanut butter.

Before bed: Have one more protein drink.

Alright, your done. Don't be fooled into thinking this is an easy workout because it's not and by the time 3:00 pm comes around, your arms are going to feel like jelly. When your arms are screaming for you to stop, your going to have to blast through.

Recovery:

This is vitally important. Recover days are just, if not more, important as the days spent preparing for your arm blitz. You should be keeping your protein intake around 1.5 to 2 grams per pound of bodyweight per day. So if you weight 175 pounds, you should be taking in about 260 to 350 grams of protein per day. You should be doing this for at least 4 days after your arm blitz routine.

Keep up the creatine intake. One to two serving per day should do the trick.

Make sure you get plenty of rest. Quality sleep is very important to the success of the arm blitz program so no late nights and get plenty of sleep. Now, you might have a hard time with this next point but you must not workout for 4 days after your arm blitz routine.

Your going to have to make sure your arms are totally recovered and draw on every resource your body has to complete the recovery of muscle fibres you've destroyed in your arms.

I have to say this again...Remember to get quality sleep. Your body has the chance to recover and grow at this crucial time so no late nights with little sleep.

Now, after 5 days after the arm blitz, measure your arms again. You should see some serious gains. This one day program will challenge even the hardest of the hardcore but the dividends are well worth the effort.

Remember, you should only do this routine once every month or your risk overtraining.

Now, if you truly want a pair of massive arms, you might want to check out the site below. You could quickly turn those scrawny average looking arms to "tree trunk" looking pipes in less time than you ever thought possible.

Lesson 2 -

How To Effectively Train Your Arms For Maximum Development

Today, I'm going to let you in on a little secret for building big arms. First, let me tell you a quick story about how I "used" to train my arms. When I first started to train arms, I wanted to lift just like Arnold did, especially the way he used to do the "cheat" curls.

You might want to stay tuned for my next email because I'm going to provide you with a mass building eating plan for workout and non workout days. Your going to have to eat a lot of quality nutrients if you want to build big arms and this meal plan will definitely help.

Lesson 3 -
"Lifting Tempo For Building Big Arms"

When it comes to building muscle mass, lifting tempo is a very important element. You want to ensure that your movements properly stimulate the targeted muscle group, in the most effective manner possible. Remember, every repetition must have a purpose, whether it be for speed, power, or building muscle and you have to lift according to that purpose.

We want to build muscle mass - This is our purpose. We must match our lifting tempo in order to effectively build quality muscle mass. In order to accomplish this, we need to understand one thing and that's to learn to control the weight in all aspects of the repetition. Each repetition must be smooth and in control so that we can keep constant tension on the muscle and ensure proper stimulation of that targeted group. This is the key.

You also have to understand that your lifting tempo must allow you to properly stretch the muscle group and to provide you with the proper range of motion. Does this mean going super slow? No, not necessarily. The thing you have to understand is "proper muscle stimulation". You see, there are two stages to an exercise, there's the lifting part (Concentric - moving the weight upwards) and the lowering of the weight (Eccentric).

Both, concentric and eccentric contractions involve somewhat different body mechanics. Think of it this way, when you lift the weight, your muscles are contracting (shortening) and when you lower the weight, your muscles are elongating.

Each part of the movement must allow for complete control in order to get the most from both, the concentric and eccentric part of the movement. This means:

• No cheating to get the weight up (This negates the positive effects of the concentric part of the movement)

• No dropping the weight down (This negates the positive effects of the eccentric part of the movement)

Each part of the movement must allow control, which means, no dropping the weight downward after performing the lifting part. This is a huge mistake which can basically cut your gains in half. The weight must be powered up, in a controlled manner and lowered in a manner that allows for complete control and stretch for total muscle stimulation.

This means, no cheating the weight up in an uncontrolled manner and no effortlessly dropping the weight down to it's starting position.

What about counting, such as counting to 3 on the way up, pause and count to 3 and than count to 4 while lowering the weight. Personally, I don't like to count when I'm doing my repetitions. If you can remember smooth and controlled on the way up and smooth and controlled on the way down, you'll do just fine.

Your lifting tempo should allow you to perform the exercise in a smooth and controlled manner while **allowing you to attain the targeted repetition range**. Remember:

• Smooth and controlled on the way up;
• Slight pause at the top;
• Smooth and controlled on the way down;
• Slight pause and repeat

Also remember this very important point. Each repetition must be performed with strict purpose that allows for complete control of the weight. Keep this in mind when you are performing your repetitions.

A Killer Arm Workout Routine

This program is all about your arms. It's going to blow up your entire arm which means your biceps, triceps and the forearm.

Optimized Nutrition Volume, 3: **building big biceps**

First of all, you will begin stretching your biceps and triceps by doing some chin-ups and push ups do about 7 reps. After you've finished the warm up, it's time to start the work.

Start with the biceps

Exercise #1

Get a barbell and load it with enough weight for you to do barbell 21's, the superset it with triceps lying dumbbells extensions do 12 quality reps.

Repeat the exercise 3 more times.

Take a short rest and than do the next exercise.

Exercise #2

Get a dumbbell and do 12 reps of dumbbells concentration curls and then superset them with standing triceps extensions

Repeat the exercise 3 more times.

Take a short rest and than do the next exercise.

Exercise #3

Do hammer curls for 8 reps and superset them with standing triceps push downs for 8 reps.
Repeat this exercise 3 more times.

Take a short rest and than off to do forearms.

For the forearms I have a killer routine that will blow your forearms up.

Exercise #1

First, do seated wrist curls and superset them with standing wrist roller. Do this for 3 sets of 12 to 15 reps After each set go to the hand gripper and grip it 12 reps and then close it for 30 seconds.

Exercise #2

Do reverse biceps curls and superset them with zottman curls do 3 sets of 12 reps

Ultimate Bicep Workout

Optimized Nutrition Volume, 3: building big biceps

The following bicep workout is an incredible outside the box approach that will shock your arms to huge gains and vein thrashing pumps. Many people working out their biceps stick with the same boring approach, and thus do not build big and muscular arms.

If you want to build some incredible biceps and have those chiseled arms you see on a fitness model or bodybuilder, you have to push yourself outside your comfort zone both mentally and physically.

This workout will train your biceps and shock your arms in a way they have never been shocked before. The results will be incredible arms and huge gains!

The ultimate bicep workout will utilize some of the best approaches to muscle building such as the drop set, super set and forced negative. Lets get started; we have some biceps to pump up!

Exercise One:

Heavy Hammer Curls with super set Palms up Dumbbell Curl

Repetitions: 10 – 12 repetitions per Set

Sets: 3

Amount of Rest between Sets: 90 Seconds

Description: This is an incredible superset because it focuses on two different parts of your bicep. You will begin the super set performing heavy hammer curls. That is, the dumbbell bicep curl where your palms are facing in. For the super set, you will grab a lighter pair of dumbbells, rotate your palms up, and perform 10-12 repetitions. You should pick a weight for both exercises that cause you to fail around the 10-12-repetition range.

Exercise Two:

E-z Bar Curl 21's

Repetitions: 7:7:7 Per Set – 21 total per set.

Optimized Nutrition Volume, 3: **building big biceps**

Sets: 3

Amount of Rest between Sets: 90 Seconds

Description: This is one of the best bicep workouts because it is a tri set that involves 21 total repetitions per set. This means that you will maximize your time under tension and really break down your muscle fibers. This means growth! To perform the ez bar curl 21's, grab an ez bar that is about half the weight of your bicep curl max. Keep a shoulder width grip, and for the 1 st 7 repetitions perform a curl where you stop halfway, forming a 90-degree angle with your forearm and upper arm.

The next 7 repetitions you will be starting at the top of the movement by your face, and lowering the weight and stopping at the exact same halfway point, with your arm bent at a 90-degree angle. For the last 7 repetitions you will be performing the complete curl. Switch-up the order for the last 2 sets and good luck – this one burns!

Example:

EZ bar curls 21's

Optimized Nutrition Volume, 3: building big biceps

Biceps And Triceps Workout To Help Build Up Those Arms

For this month's workout, I've decided to go ahead with a biceps and triceps workout.

It's a pretty straight forward workout that targets the the muscles of the upper arms with key movements designed to stimulate the key muscle fibres.

I suggest you try this workout for a month or so until you see the desired results.

I also suggest you train biceps and triceps together because it seems more natural to train them both in one session.

However, if you are currently training biceps on another training day, try mixing it up and train arms on the same day for a month or so.

You can use this workout with another body parts such as chest or shoulders but if you truly want a pair of big arms, I suggest you train them on a day of they're own. That is, give them special attention (specialization).

If your not familiar with specialization or prioritization, it simply means to make that particular exercise or body part the number one priority in your weight training routine.

For example, let's say you want to improve your squat.

By prioritizing that exercise, you give it your complete focus and effort.

What you would do is make the squat the number one exercise in your routine that's trained first in your workout cycle.

More than likely, you would train legs by themselves and with no other body part so you can give it total effort. This is specialization and it's a technique you should become familiar with.

Anyways, I'll leave it up to you as to whether or not you want to train them on a different day than your other body parts.

Let's take a look at the workout:

The Workout

Biceps:

Seated Alternate Dumbbell Curls

Warm up: 1 x 20 repetitions;
Set 1: 1 x 12 repetitions;
Set 2: 1 x 10 repetitions;
Set 3: 1 x 8 repetitions;
Set 4: 1 x 6 - 8 repetitions.

From sets 1 to 4, you should be increasing the weight until you can just get 8 repetitions for the last set. Lets say, I know that my max curl weight is 70 pounds (dumbbell). My repetitions scheme will be as follows:

Warm up: 20 pound dumbbells for 20 repetitions;
Set 1: 30 pound for 10 reps;
Set 2: 40 pounds for 8 reps;
Set 3: 50 pounds for 8 reps;
Set 4: 60 pounds for 6 - 8 reps;

You should rest about 50 seconds in between each set. Once you've finished your last set, head on over to the barbell rack.

Standing Barbell Curls

I've put a different spin on the barbell curl. Instead of taking a 40 to 60 second rest in between each set, you're going to only be resting to the count of 10. This method really boosts the intensity of this exercise and it will cause your biceps to really burn. For the first couple of workouts, your biceps and forearms are going to scream in agony, but after wards, they will start get stronger. Once your arms start to get accustomed to the weight, try increasing the poundage by 10 - Usually every two weeks. Here is the repetitions scheme:

4 x 8 repetitions

What you want to do here is pick a weight that you know you can do 12 reps with. Once you have the weight you wish to use, set it down and get a drink of water. Here's what I want you to do:

Set 1: Perform 8 repetitions, put the weight down and count to 10. Once you've finished counting to 10, go onto set 2.

Set 2: Perform 8 repetitions, put the weight down and count to 10. Once you've finished counting to 10, go onto set 3.

Set 3: Perform 8 repetitions, put the weight down and count to 10. Once you've finished counting to 10, go onto set 4.

Set 4: Perform 8 repetitions, put the weight down and take a drink of water.

Your arms should be burning and very tight. If they're not, increase the weight by 5 to 10 pounds. Take a 30 second rest and head on over to the preacher bench.

Preacher Curls

3 x 10 repetitions

Preacher curls make for a nice finishing move because they really stretch your biceps out. There is nothing fancy about this exercise so it's a straight 3 sets. Pick a weight that you can do a hard 10 repetitions with. Try resting about 30 seconds in between each set.

After you've completed the last set, take a 30 second breather and head on over to the bench press. It's time to do triceps.

Triceps:

Close Grip Bench Press

Warm up: 1 x 20 repetitions;
Set 1: 1 x 8 repetitions;
Set 2: 1 x 8 repetitions;
Set 3: 1 x 6 repetitions;
Set 4: 1 x 6 repetitions;
Set 5: 1 x 12 repetitions.

The close grip bench press is a compound movement meant to add power and muscle to your triceps. Want you want to do here is add weight with each progressive set. For example, let's say your max close grip bench press is 200 pounds. For your warm up, your going to use about 45% of your max which would be about 90 - 95 pounds.

You should be able to complete an easy 20 repetitions. For your second set, your going to use about 60% of your max which, in this case, is about 120 pounds. Rest for about 60 seconds and do your second set.

For your second set, you should be using about 70% of your max, which in this example is about 140 pounds. Complete 8 repetitions and rest for another 60 seconds.

For your third set, your going to use 80% of your max and complete 6 repetitions. For this example, the weight will be about 160 pounds. Rest for another 60 seconds. For your final set, your going to use about 85% of your max. In this example, the weight will be around 170 pounds. As soon as you've completed the set, count to 15 and lighten the weight to about 65% of your max and complete 12 repetitions. These repetitions should be done very, very slowly. Really concentrate on the pushing portion of the exercise during this set.

Since you are using heavier weights with this exercise, you should get a spotter for sets 3 and 4. You don't want to be stuck on the bench press with a barbell on your chest!

Rest for about 30 seconds and head on over to the cable press down machine (or lat machine).

Cable Press Downs

3 x 12 repetitions

This is a pretty straightforward exercise. You will want to make sure you do this exercise in super strict fashion. Perform the exercises slowly and in a controlled manner. Remember, keep the elbows in and squeeze at the bottom of the movement. Rest for about 30 seconds in between each set and try to increase the weight with each set, as well. That is, pyramid the weight from sets 1 through 3.

Once you've completed the cable press downs, head on over to the barbell rack.

Standing (Or Seated) French Presses

I find the standing French barbell press a great finishing movement for the triceps. As you can see in the image above, the exercise is perform sitting down. However, I prefer to stand up to do this exercise. If you are new to this movement, pick a light barbell that you know is light and press it over your head and lower the weight, while keeping your elbows elevated (as in the image above).

The repetitions scheme is as follows:

3 x 12 repetitions

I personally like to pyramid the weight up. However, this exercise is about form and you need to choose a weight that will allow you to perform 12 repetitions in strict manner. I suggest you try and use a light weight for your first set and rest for about 30 seconds. If you feel the weight was pretty light and performed the repetitions in strict form, try using a heavier weight. Rest for about 30 seconds and perform the final set.

If there is one thing that I strongly suggest you do is to eat every two to three hours. Now, you don't have to eat a full blown meal. The important thing is to eat. Carry a pack sack around with you and have apples, bananas, granola bars, protein drinks and some vegetables. This way your always feeding your body.

For an even more detailed look at putting together a targeted nutritional plan, try using Will Brink's Muscle Building Nutrition. This book will cover every detail of putting together your nutritional plan, step by step. Will is a world renowned author on sports nutrition and his book will definitely help you put together a true muscle building nutritional plan

How To Build Bigger Triceps

Here's an email I received from a reader wanting to know if training chest and triceps on the same day is an effective workout for the triceps:

Question:

"Would you recommend doing flat bench, close-grip bench, and triceps all on the same day, or would you say that splitting those exercises up might be more effective? Any advice you could pass along would be greatly appreciated by my students and I. Thank you for the articles and your time."

Answer:

Personally, I've trained chest and arms on the same day for years. Here's one of my sample routines:

Chest:

bench press
Incline dumbbell press
Incline fly

Superset biceps and triceps

Close grip bench press superset with standing barbell curls
Standing cable press downs superset with standing alternate curls
Overhead french press superset with preacher curls

I've had plenty of success with this type of routine. For me, chest and arms go along perfectly. However, you may find training chest and triceps on the same day to taxing on your triceps. Personally, most of these exercises are pushing movements so they fit well with each other.

You see, triceps can easily get over trained. I'd rather train triceps no more than 2 times per week for direct and indirect movements. Anymore than 2 times and your increasing your chances of overtraining your triceps. I've tried a bunch of combinations for split training and the best one (for me) is chest and arms. I like to train my triceps hard on day one and hit them once more, two to three days afterwards for indirect movements such as with shoulder press'

You see, by the time day 4 comes along, which is my shoulder day, my triceps are stronger, and well rested. This is what I want because my shoulder strength is very dependant on my triceps strength. Weak and sore triceps means weak pressing movements which means no muscle improvements.

Of course everyone is different. My shoulders are much stronger than my triceps are and can take much more punishment but my triceps are easily over trained. Once my triceps go, everything goes.

Here's what it all boils down to - Recuperation times.

You don't build muscle in the gym, you actually tear down your muscle tissue in the gym. The muscle repairs itself while it's resting, and that process starts as soon as you hit the showers after your training session. Want to know what the true muscle builder is? It's your recuperation time.

If you can find the right rest combination, you'll have a true muscle building routine. I've tried training my triceps on different days and for some reason, they are always sore and tired. I have found that if I train my triceps hard on day one with chest, they are well rested and stronger by the time shoulders come around which is usually on day 4. I indirectly train my triceps on day 4 and by the time day one comes around, which is usually the following Monday, my triceps are ready for heavy training again.

Basically, I will hit my triceps directly, once per week, and indirectly, once per week.

My suggestion is to play around with the routine and find the best rest periods for optimal growth. The thing you have to remember is that everyone is different. What may work for me, might not work for you so you have to do a little bit of experimenting to find your optimal rest times.

Optimized Nutrition Volume, 3: building big biceps

Section 2: Biceps

4 Moves to Bring Your Biceps to New Heights

As a trainer, one of the most common queries I receive in regards to body part troubleshooting is, "how can I achieve a better peak on my biceps?"

The fact that some people develop longer, more football shaped biceps, while others develop shorter, more mountain-like biceps is mostly a matter left up to genetics. But do not fear, because there's a way that EVERYONE can create the illusion of having a **more substantial biceps peak**!

Reach Your Biceps Peak

The key lies in bringing about greater development in a little-discussed muscle that sits underneath the biceps called the brachialis. In a highly defined bodybuilder, the brachialis appears as a thick "knot" of muscle that pops out of the side of the upper arm when they are flexed and viewed from the rear. The cool thing about the brachialis is that as it grows larger, it will actually "**push" the biceps up higher**, which will give the appearance of a greater peak!

The problem with effectively stimulating the brachialis is that with most standard curling movements the biceps act as the main flexor of the upper arm. You need to choose specific curling exercises that put the biceps in a mechanically weak position, so that the brachialis can get into the game! The more work you can force the brachialis to take on, the more it will be forced to adapt and grow.

The following exercises are custom made to attack the brachialis, allowing you to move a few steps closer to hitting that biceps peak!

4 Moves to Bring Your Biceps to New Heights

Hammer Curls

Grab a pair of dumbbells and hold them at your sides with your palms facing inward toward your thighs. Curl the dumbbells together, but keep your palms facing inward throughout the set, as if using a hammer. Make sure to keep your elbows locked in place, not allowing them to rise up or outward while you curl. At the peak contraction point squeeze extra hard before slowly lowering the dumbbells back to arms length.

Add some elevation to your cannons with these targeted bicep exercises.

Reverse Curls

These are performed just like regular barbell curls with the only exception being that the palms are facing down. The palms down position will force the brachialis and the brachioradialis of the forearm to work intensely during this movement. Make sure you keep your elbows locked into your sides, and wrists straight throughout the set.

Keep the weight moderate and the reps in the 10-12 range. If you find that doing reverse curls with a straight bar is uncomfortable, try using an EZ-curl bar instead.

Add some elevation to your cannons with these targeted bicep exercises.

90-Degree Preacher Curl

With this movement you will be curling off of the vertical, not angled, side of a preacher bench. Load up a barbell with only about 60-70% of your normal preacher curl weight. Position yourself over the bench in such a manner that your armpits are snugly pressed into the top. Grab the weight and allow your arms to hang straight down.

As you start to curl make sure that your shoulders and elbows remain locked in position, so that the brachialis is forced to work as hard as possible to flex the arm. At the top of the movement squeeze tightly. Slowly lower the bar back to the starting position.

Add some elevation to your cannons with these targeted bicep exercises.

Overhead Cable Curls

This unique exercise is my personal favorite for a targeted assault on the brachialis. Place a flat bench in front of a weight stack on one side of a cable crossover machine. Make sure that the bench is at least a foot or so away from the stack. Attach a short straight bar to the upper pulley, lie down, and plant your feet firmly on the floor. Have someone hand you the bar.

Start with your arms perfectly straight and then begin curling the bar both down *and* back, so that at the full contraction point, the bar is actually behind your head. As you curl you will need to draw your elbows back slightly and tip your head forward just a bit in order to achieve this exaggerated range of motion. At the bottom hold the squeeze for a count and then return the bar under control to the starting position.

Hit the Smaller Muscles With This Better Biceps Workout

When it comes to **arm training**, one muscle in particular always seems to hog the spotlight. The biceps brachii is the large two-headed muscle that makes up much of your upper arm, but it doesn't work alone.

The brachialis and brachioradialis muscles, which help flex the elbow joint, also contribute size and shape to the pipes, though it takes a little extra manipulation to get them to grow. The brachioradialis makes up a good part of your forearm as well and will complete your arm development by adding a Popeye-like lower arm to bulging, **bigger biceps**. In other words, biceps training isn't just about training the biceps.

ARM YOURSELF

Most people start their biceps routine with a straight **bar curl**, arguably the best mass-building move there is for the bodypart. But starting there fatigues some of the smaller muscles of the arm, making it hard to get them to respond later in your routine and thus hampering long term mass gains.

Although most research would argue against working smaller muscles first, this may be your best option because it stimulates all the elbow flexors and increases total muscle recruitment right out of the box.

Remember, muscles eventually get bored by the same old workout. They learn to be more efficient, and they just flat out quit growing in the absence of new challenges. By working smaller muscles first in your workout, you burn them out and require the larger muscles to work even harder to recruit more muscle fibers.

And while this may seem contrary to the physiological standards for muscle expression, continual stress forces continual recruitment, which should translate into greater strength and size gains in the long run.

You know the adage: Insanity is doing the same thing over and over and expecting a different result. When you aim to improve your physique, you don't use the same approach day after day; instead, you diversify, incorporating several different movements, angles and loads. And when something stops working for you in the gym, common sense dictates that it's time for a change. Yet there are some who play to the adage, repeating the failed workouts of yesteryear in hopes that this time will be different. One of the joys of lifting weights is that you have hundreds of options at your disposal, and there may be no greater ally than dumbbells in the quest for a better body.

Dumbbells are the Talented Mr. Ripley of the fitness world, doing the work of barbells and machines in nearly every imaginable exercise, oftentimes better. Their versatility is second to none, allowing lifters to detect muscular imbalances, train without a spotter, vary wrist angles...the list goes on. This month, take a mostly unilateral approach to your biceps training. Open with a standard mass-builder, dumbbell-style. From there, it's on to dumbbell incline curls, which target the outer head of your bi's. Close with a one-arm **preacher curl** to bombard that often-neglected inner head.

Need to inject a little variety into your **biceps workout**? Then walk away from that rack of EZ-bars and try our all-dumbbell routine. You'll work your peaks from different positions that are guaranteed to keep them growing.

1. Standing Dumbbell Curl

How Many? 1 warm-up + 4 sets; 10, 10, 12, 12 reps

1) START: Stand erect holding two dumbbells at your sides. Maintain a slight bend in your elbows. Palms face forward.

2) MOVE: In an explosive yet controlled manner, simultaneously curl both dumbbells, keeping your elbows tight at your sides. At the top, squeeze your biceps hard as you hold the peak contraction momentarily. Slowly reverse the motion, bringing the weights back to the start. Repeat.

2. Incline Alternating Dumbbell Curl

How Many? 4 sets; 8-12 reps apiece

1) START: Set the bench to about a 45-60-degree angle. Hold a dumbbell in each hand as you sit back on the bench and allow your arms to hang straight down toward the floor. Palms faced forward.

2) MOVE: Curl one arm at a time toward the same-side shoulder, keeping your elbow back. Keep your head straight and don't lean to either side. Squeeze your biceps at the top. Slowly lower to the start. Alternate arms.

3. One-Arm Dumbbell Preacher Curl

How Many? 3 sets; 10-15 reps for each arm

1) START: Hold a dumbbell in one hand and secure yourself on a preacher bench. Keep your nonworking hand on the bench for balance.

2) MOVE: Slowly lower the dumbbell, stopping just short of locking out your elbow. In a smooth and controlled motion, curl the weight toward the same-side shoulder. Squeeze at the top before slowly returning to the start. Complete all reps for one side, then repeat with the opposite arm.

Build bigger arms by bringing more muscle to bear on the weight being moved with these atypical arm-day selections.

Barbell curls. **Preachers**. Extensions. Press downs. On arm day, these are a few of our favorite things. But these moves are single-joint moves that **isolate your biceps** and triceps. Larger muscle groups, such as the chest, back and quads, are usually bombarded with an array of multi-joint moves that allow for more weight before isolation exercises come into play. Is it possible to use that same strategy on your arms? Justin Grinnell, CSCS, owner of State of Fitness, believes it is.

"When athletes think about developing ripped arms, they immediately think of isolation exercises, such as biceps curls and triceps press downs," he says. "While isolation movements are great when trying to add some detail to a muscle group, for overall mass and strength gains, **compound movements** will always trump isolation movements."

Grinnell says that multi-joint moves and heavier weight loads will lead to a greater release of your body's natural growth hormone (GH), testosterone and IGF-1. Collectively, these hormones work to help you add size…everywhere. That includes your pipes. Just train, feed and repeat. Here are Grinnell's four moves to get you going.

Build bigger arms by bringing more muscle to bear on the weight being moved with these atypical arm-day selections.

Target: Biceps

When was the last time you did a full set of chin-ups to failure? If you have, then you are likely familiar with the ache in your biceps' bellies the next day. Turns out, it's not really just a back exercise. Not by a long shot.

"Your biceps have to work so hard to grip and pull your elbow into flexion that there is a tremendous amount of muscle tissue that is stimulated."

Grinnell says to grip a pull-up bar underhand with your palms six inches apart and, starting from a dead hang, "pull yourself up until your upper-chest comes in contact with the bar." Pause for a full second and the top, and lower yourself slowly until your arms become totally straight. Pulling yourself up all the way to the bar, Grinnell says, slightly increases the range of motion and thus the demand placed on the biceps.

Build bigger arms by bringing more muscle to bear on the weight being moved with these atypical arm-day selections.

target: Biceps

You likely already do hammer curls in your routine but *hammer rows*? Grinnell says to think of it as a modified concentration curl, where you're getting a bit of help from your back to complete heavier-than-normal reps of an already effective biceps exercise.

"Grab a dumbbell that you can usually row for about 15 reps," he says. "Assume the same position as a standard one-arm dumbbell row. Instead of pulling straight back, as you do when rowing, you will perform a hammer curl as you pull the dumbbell to the top, near your pecs. Pause and squeeze your biceps and then lower slowly until your arm is fully extended. Due to your position and the support from your back muscles, you are able to put more stress on the biceps due to the increased weight being use. Your upper-back will be fried as a byproduct."

Build bigger arms by bringing more muscle to bear on the weight being moved with these atypical arm-day selections.

One of the most beneficial yet underused exercises for building bulging triceps is the dip. Because it calls your delts and pecs into play to complete each rep, you are able to more effectively overload the triceps. And if you get to the point where you can add resistance, then you're in for some serious size. But if you have the opportunity to use rings, you can reap additional rewards.

"The added instability causes your triceps and supporting muscles to work harder to complete each rep," says Grinnell. "In the absence of rings, standard dips will still add serious mass. They may not be the biggest guys but gymnasts have some of the best-looking arms in the world."

Big, Burly, Badass Biceps
Fire up your guns with these arm blasting bi-laws.

If *your* biceps are not quite where you want them to be despite your most ferocious efforts in the gym, read on, and maybe you will run across a *bi-law* that will help get the job done for you.

Bend 'Em Back

Trainees often tell me that when they work their biceps, their forearms get the more intense pump. That's not a good thing if you're looking for **bigger guns**. If that sounds like you, then what you should actually be doing during most curling movements is bending your wrists *back* and holding that position throughout the set. That effectively takes the forearm flexors out of the movement, forcing the biceps to do almost all of the work.

Yes, it will feel a little odd at first—and chances are your curling poundage will drop somewhat—but trust me when I tell you that you will actually **hit your biceps harder** than ever before. Try using this method on at least one exercise in each biceps workout (I suggest a barbell movement), and I bet you'll see improvements.

Keep Your Chin-Up

When I talk about your "chin," I'm not referring to the one on your face, but the kind you should be doing in the gym if you want to pummel those biceps into growth. Close-grip, underhand chins are one of the most effective biceps exercises you can do; yet few trainees ever use them. To get the most out of your close-grip chins, make sure you use perfect form. I recommend spacing your hands no wider than six inches apart.

Begin the movement at a dead hang, with your arms completely straight. At the peak of the concentric portion of the rep your chin should rise just above the bar (no half-reps please) as you squeeze your bi's hard. Try to lower yourself very slowly, taking up to four to six seconds to get to the bottom position. When you can get 10 to 12 reps with your bodyweight, add some extra resistance with a belt designed to hold plates and/or a dumbbell around your waist. Once you're doing clean reps with 50 extra pounds attached to you, your biceps will have all the mass you could ever want.

Twice Is Nice

It's very much in vogue these days to train each body part only once per week, and with good reason: It works. When you're looking for some extra growth in a particular muscle, however, it can be very effective to hit that muscle twice per week for a time. The keys to an effective two-days-per-week biceps-prioritization program are: 1) Make sure there are at least three days between workouts, and 2) do two different types of workouts each week. Here's a split that you can use while doing two biceps workouts per week:

Monday: Chest and biceps
Tuesday: Quads and hams
Thursday: Lats and traps
Friday: Shoulders, biceps and triceps

With a program like this, I suggest you make Monday your main biceps day, using about a third more volume—that is, sets—than you use on Friday. It can also be very effective to use heavier weights and lower reps in one workout and lighter weights and higher reps in the next. Another way I like to vary the two biceps workouts is to use all barbell movements the first day and all dumbbell movements the next. That's something you can experiment with, as long as there are some meaningful variations between the two workouts.

Go Angling

Change your lines of pull, body position and/or planes of motion in order to stimulate your biceps in ways they aren't used to. That will change motor recruitment patterns, wake up the central nervous system and even enable you to preferably recruit the inner or outer biceps head to a greater degree. Here are some ways to use this concept:

•Instead of curling off of the angled side of a preacher bench, curl off of the vertical side.

Optimized Nutrition Volume, 3: building big biceps

- Instead of doing seated DB curls, try incline DB curls. If you already do those, try going for a steeper angle.
- When doing DB curls of any kind, try grabbing the 'bells by either the inside or outside plates rather than in the middle. That alone will change how the movement affects the biceps.
- When using a barbell, vary your grip from wide to narrow.
- When using DB's, try either curling across your body or turning your palms out and curling away from your body.
- Try sitting at an upper-pulley cable station and curling a straight bar back behind your head.
- Try lying down at a seated cable row station and doing curls while flat on your back.

Grow With Slow-Mo

It has been my observation that most guys do their curls with a tempo of 1/0/1/0. If you're not familiar with that method of expressing lifting speed, it simply means that the eccentric, or negative, portion of the lift is completed in one second; there's no pause at the bottom; the concentric, or positive, portion of the lift is completed in one second; and there is no pause at the top. At that tempo each rep takes approximately two seconds to complete, and since most sets are anywhere from six to 10 reps, the time under tension (TUT) will only be 12 to 20 seconds.

That's not enough for those looking to stimulate hypertrophy in a muscle. Studies have shown that the optimal TUT for gains in muscle size is 40 to 70 seconds per set. My suggestion to anyone seeking more size on their bi's is a repetition tempo of 3/1/2/1, which will bring the length of each rep to seven seconds. That translates to a TUT of 42 to 70 seconds for sets of six to 12 reps. Perfect!

4 Arm Exercises For Bigger Biceps
Train your biceps from all angles – and hit your forearms while you're at it – with this arm workout.

Being a former Goldern Gloves-contending boxer, Manhattan-based trainer Clay Burwell knows a thing or two about training arms. When it comes to **building big biceps**, you can't really stray from doing some sort of curl, but that doesn't mean you can't vary your workouts with any number of curling offshoots. In the below Burwell-designed routine, two bodybuilding staples (incline dumbbell curls and **cable curls**) are grouped with **TRX** curls, where you lift your bodyweight up using only your biceps.

This combination of free weight training, the constant tension provided by cables and a gymnastics-like strength move will provide a spark to help bring up even the most stubborn of biceps peaks. And because no good pair of arms is complete without adequate forearm and grip strength, Burwell threw in a grueling farmer's walk with four dangling kettlebells. Expect some next-day arm soreness after this one.

BICEPS & GRIP WORKOUT

Exercise	Sets	Reps
Unilateral Cable Curl	3	8
Incline Dumbbell Curl	4	10
TRX Curl	3	8
Figure-8 4-Kettlebell Farmer's Walk	2	10 laps

See next page for tips on how to best perform these moves.

Unilateral Cable Curl

Burwell's Tip: "For variety, try using no attachment handle. Grip it by the rubber stopper and step back about five feet from the stack. The cable angle will add resistance at the top of the movement and the hammer grip offers more emphasis on the brachioradialis muscle."

Incline Dumbbell Curl

Burwell's Tip: "Make sure you maintain a dead hang in your arms with your elbows pointed at the ground throughout. At the top, hold the contraction for two seconds."

TRX Curl

Burwell's Tip: "Your upper arm should be perpendicular to your torso, and there should be a 90-degree angle at your armpit."

Figure-8 4-Kettlebell Farmer's Walk

Place two five-pound plates on the floor about 15 feet apart. Select two heavy kettlebells (32-50 kg) and two lighter ones (8 kg is ideal). Hold one light and one heavy kettlebell in each hand and walk in a figure-8 pattern around the five-pound plates. Do 10 laps total. If you can do more than 10 laps with relative ease, use heavier kettlebells.

Add Inches To Your Biceps with 21s

Build up some bigger arm artillery with this killer bicep move.

To really allow your biceps to reach their full potential you may need to start adding 21's to your **biceps' routine.** The number "21" refers to the number of total reps you do in one set. However, this particular "21" is divided into three 7-rep segments that ultimately target the entire bicep.

1st 7 Reps: For the first seven reps, go from the bottom of the movement up to the halfway point (with your arms at a 90 degree angle and hands at elbow level).

2nd 7 Reps: Go from the halfway point up to the top of the **bicep curl** (hands up near shoulder level).

3rd 7 Reps: Start at the bottom of the movement and complete a full range of movement all the way up.

How To Perform 21s

- Stand upright and grab a barbell with an underhand grip.
- Place your hands shoulders-width apart and allow your arms to hang toward the floor.
- Tuck your elbows tight to the sides of your body.
- Curl upward until you make a 90-degree angle at your elbow.
- Relax your arms back to full extension and repeat six more curls reaching the 90-degree angle at your elbow.
- Now, from the 90-degree at your elbow position, curl the weight up until the barbell is one to two inches away from your shoulder.
- Lower the weight back to the 90-degree elbow position and repeat six more times.
- Now, allow your arms to return to full extension.
- This time, curl your arms from full extension all the way to full extension. Keep curling until the bar is about one to two inches away from your shoulder.
- Repeat six more curls through this full range of motion to complete a total of 21 curls.

15 Minutes to Bigger Arms

Grow your guns even when you're short on time with this hard-hitting (and brief) biceps/triceps routine

It doesn't take long to blast your arms and spark new gun growth. The below six exercises are to be performed as two separate giant sets (three exercises per giant set) repeated twice, which, according to my math (see below) will take you a mere 15 minutes. All the best mass-building moves for arms are included here—from chins to dips to close-grip bench. To maximize efficiency, set up all of the exercises/stations before you start the workout so you can transition quickly between them.

The Workout -

EXERCISE	REPS	REST
Chin-ups	8	30-seconds
Dips	8-12	30-seconds
Cable Triceps Extension	20	30-seconds

Perform two times through.

EXERCISE	REPS	REST
Close-Grip Bench Press	6-8	30-seconds
Reverse-Grip EZ-Bar Curl	8-12	30-seconds
Two-Arm Dumbbell Curl	8-12	30-seconds

Perform two times through.

The Math:
First Giant Set
1A) 4 sec. per rep x 8 reps + 30 sec. rest = 62 seconds
1B) 3 sec. per rep x 12 reps + 30 sec. rest = 66 seconds
1C) 3 sec. per rep x 20 reps + 30 sec. rest = 90 seconds
SUBTOTAL: 218 seconds = 3.63 min x 2 rounds = 7.27 minutes
Second Giant Set
2A) 4 sec. per rep x 8 reps + 30 sec. rest = 62 seconds
2B) 3 sec. per rep x 12 reps + 30 sec. rest = 66 seconds
2C) 3 sec. per rep x 12 reps + 30 sec. rest = 66 seconds
SUBTOTAL: 194 seconds = 3.23 min x 2 rounds = 6.47 minutes
TOTAL: 13.74 minutes (15 minutes with time transitioning between exercises)

Coaching Cues:

CHIN-UPS

Control the tempo and don't swing.

Keep tension on the biceps and lats the entire set.

Don't relax at the bottom of the movement; this strains the shoulders and makes it hard to reverse the movement.

Squeeze the biceps tight at the top of the movement.

Overload with a dip belt and dumbbell if you're strong enough.

If the chin-ups strain your elbows, try different hand widths – i.e., a closer hand position helps alleviate stress.

DIPS

Lean forward to lessen the strain on the shoulders and keep tension on the chest and triceps.

Lower until the arm angle is 90 degrees or the triceps are parallel to the floor.

Overload with dip belt and dumbbell if you're strong enough.

CABLE TRICEPS EXTENSION

Keep torso leaning slightly forward.

Don't throw the weight; keep the movement smooth.

Drive each rep to lockout.

CLOSE-GRIP BENCH PRESS

Elbows should be tucked to sides.

Place middle finger on the end of the knurling.

Keep chest up to lessen strain on shoulders at the bottom of the movement (bar on the chest).

Keep shoulders pulled back and down (retraction and depression).

Drive feet downward into the floor to keep full body tension.

Keep tension throughout the lift and don't bounce the bar off your chest.

REVERSE-GRIP EZ-BAR CURL

Pull your shoulders back.

Don't swing the weight.

Keep elbows fixed at your sides.

If the movement strains your elbows, try taking your thumbs and putting them behind the bar with your fingers.

TWO-ARM DUMBBELL CURL

Control the tempo and don't swing the weight.

Keep the elbows fixed diagonally outward.

Curl both dumbbells up at the same (as opposed to one at a time) to save time.

Keep your head back in line with your torso.

Squeeze biceps hard at the top of the movement.

6 Tips for Decked Out Arms

1. I determine my weight loads on a workout-by-workout basis; it just depends on how I feel that day. You should train with logic and reason, and that means going by your energy levels and listening to your body. I train as heavy as I feel I can possibly go on a particular day.

2. At this stage in my career, I never really change my exercises around too much. I've found what works best for me and what my arms respond to. But if I'm looking for more detail or shape, I'll add sets or reps to certain move-ments such as concentration curls or rope pressdowns.

3. Something that people overlook is stretching. You should stretch to make sure your muscle bellies can extend, fill with more blood and grow. Once I plateaued and started stretching my calves, for example, I found that growth in them came a little easier.

4. The first thing you need to focus on when training arms or any other bodypart is proper form. Cheating your reps is an advanced principle that should be used only later in a set. That's why seated movements are good—they eliminate your ability to swing the weight.

5. Make sure you pay attention to diet, rest and recovery; it's not all about what you do in the gym. You have to train your arms, sure, but you need to eat the proper foods after training to maximize your growth. Don't eat to feed your belly—eat to feed your muscles.

6. Don't overcomplicate your routine with too many movements and intensity techniques. I stick to basic mass-building exercises and rep ranges, although I superset occasionally to turn things up a notch.

Seated Alternating Dumbbell Curl   4[1]   10

Optimized Nutrition Volume, 3: building big biceps

Standing EZ-Bar Curl	3—4	6—8
Concentration Curl	3—4	8—10
Rope Press down	4 [2]	20—30
Seated Overhead Dumbbell Extension	4	6—8
Lying Triceps Extension	3	8—12

Arm Yourself with This Biceps-Blasting Workout

Beat your biceps into submission with this instant bulk-building routine.

Seems like everyone's out to find a newer, better way to train their biceps. **Drop sets**, weird splits and awkward exercises are all part of the trial and error guessing game. But novel training methods don't necessarily equate to shirt-busting results.

If you want big guns, you need to work them like you want them to grow. Don't stop when they're tired- hit 'em some more. The reason why most new-age "functional" trainers and trainees lack sizeable arms is that they don't hit them hard enough. Not that you should overtrain your biceps, but please feel free to exhaust them into submission every now and then. Building up your biceps involves two key ingredients: increasing the training load and making sure your muscles are exposed to a sufficient number of reps. The below routine is designed to do both.

You'll **increase biceps size and strength** by alternating between sets of higher and lower reps while increasing and decreasing the weight accordingly for a generous 14 sets per workout. And you'll finish off by grinding out two "pump sets" of 10 reps with shorter rest periods. Combine this routine with another bodypart if you dare, but if you can find time to do these mini-workouts on their own, make it so to increase the focus on your biceps and really see your efforts pay off.

After 4-6 weeks of this twice-a-week biceps regimen you should see a marked improvement. If you can, go for another couple weeks, as each additional workout will only add to your arm circumference. Remember, it takes time to see super, and the bi's are only one half of the equation (your triceps make up the other half). But if you can consistently hit your arms with volume and intensity week in, week out, biceps workouts won't be so much of a guessing game.

The Workout

Day 1

Exercise	Sets	Reps*	Rest
EZ-Bar Curl	4	12, 6, 12, 6	90 sec., 2 min., 90 sec., 2 min.
Seated Hammer Curl	4	12, 8, 12, 8	90 sec., 2 min., 90 sec., 2 min.
Cable Straight-Bar Curl	4	10, 5, 10, 5	2 min.
Single-Arm Dumbbell Preacher Curl	2	10, 10	1 min.

Day 2

Exercise	Sets	Reps*	Rest
Cable Straight-Bar Curl	4	12, 6, 12, 6	90 sec., 2 min., 90 sec., 2 min.
Single-Arm Dumbbell Preacher Curl	4	12, 8, 12, 8	90 sec., 2 min., 90 sec., 2 min.
EZ-Bar Curl	4	10, 5, 10, 5	2 min.
Seated Hammer Curl	2	10, 10	1 min.

Adjust weight accordingly – heavier weight for lower reps, lighter weight for higher reps.

Attack Your Biceps With the Lying Cable Curl

Trigger new biceps growth with this isolation move.

Few things can derail your biceps progress more than lack of exercise variety. There's pretty much only one movement you can do for the bi's (the curl), and doing only barbell and dumbbell curls can get stale. Lucky for you, we've got a cure for the boredom: the lying cable curl. Its the perfect finishing move for a workout that also includes heavy barbell and/or dumbbell curls. Include this exercise on your next arm day and you'll be a little less bored, and a lot more pumped in the biceps.

THE CURL ZONE

Follow these instructions to bring a more intense burn to your biceps via cables.

SET UP

1. Lie on the floor in a cable crossover station with your head a foot or so from the weight stack.
2. Grasp a straight- or EZ-bar attachment coming from a high pulley, setting up with a palms-up grip (forearms facing you).
3. Begin with your arms fully extended toward the ceiling, your knees bent, and feet flat on the floor.

DO IT

Keeping your upper arms completely stationary (more or less perpendicular to the floor),contract your biceps to bend your elbows and curl the bar down to your forehead.Touch down lightly, squeeze your biceps hard for one to two seconds, then slowly return to the arms-extended position

QUICK TIPS

Where It Hits: Biceps
When To Do It: At the end of your workout, after barbell and DB curls
How To Do It: 2-4 sets, 8-15 reps

Climb the Ladder for Bigger Biceps
Grow your guns with this bodyweight extended set curling exercise

Regular readers of my articles and viewers of my M&F Raw! series know that I'm a big believer in using **multijoint exercises** to encourage greater muscle growth, since these moves involve at least one other muscle group to assist the target muscle, which allows you to go heavier than you can with single joint exercises. But when it comes to biceps, none of the traditional exercises used are compound moves – until now.

A great multijoint **exercise for the biceps** that I created to force even the most stubborn arms to grow is the biceps ladder. The easiest place to do this is on a Smith machine or power rack. Set the bar in the Smith machine at a height that allows you to hang from it as if doing an inverted row so that your back just clears the floor. Use an underhand grip and pull your face up toward the bar in a curling motion, then slowly lower your body back to the start position.

Do as many reps as you can until you reach muscle failure, then immediately raise the bar up one notch and continue doing body curls. Each time you reach muscle failure, raise the bar up a notch until you've reached the top notch. Every time you raise the bar up it reduces the resistance that your body provides, making it easier to continue the set. So in essence, this is one long extended set. The novel movement of this exercise will stimulate muscle fibers that you've likely been ignoring, and this move also places a high load on the negative part of the rep (especially on the lower rungs), which induces a lot of biceps muscle damage to stimulate new growth.

Climb The Ladder Biceps Workout

Exercise	Sets	Reps	Rest
Biceps Ladder	1-3*	to failure	3 min.
Incline Dumbbell Curl	4	8-10	1-2 min.

Start off with one full set of biceps ladders. Once that's no longer challenging, bump it up to two sets, and then eventually three.

Raw Tip: On the lower rungs, where the resistance is the greatest, you may need to cheat yourself up on the positive part of the rep and focus just on the negative. Try to get at least five reps on each position, even if you have to cheat to do

Bigger Biceps, Better Grip
Train your biceps from all angles, and hit your forearms while you're at it, with this arm arsenal.

Being a former Golden Gloves-contending boxer, Manhattan-based trainer Clay Burwell knows a thing or two about training arms. When it comes to biceps, you can't really stray from doing some sort of curl, but that doesn't mean you can't vary your workouts with any number of curling offshoots. In the below Burwell-designed routine, two bodybuilding staples (incline dumbbell curls and cable curls) are grouped with TRX curls, where you lift your bodyweight up using only your biceps.

This combination of free weight training, the constant tension provided by cables and a gymnastics-like strength move will provide a spark to help bring up even the most stubborn of biceps peaks. And because no good pair of arms is complete without adequate forearm and grip strength, Burwell threw in a grueling farmer's walk with four dangling kettlebells. Expect some next-day arm soreness after this one.

Optimized Nutrition Volume, 3: building big biceps

BICEPS AND GRIP WORKOUT

Exercise	Sets	Reps
Unilateral Cable Curl	3	8
Incline Dumbbell Curl	4	10
TRX Curl	3	8
Figure-8 4-Kettlebell Farmer's Walk	2	10 laps

Burwell's Tip for Unilateral Cable Curl: "For variety, try using no attachment handle. Grip it by the rubber stopper and step back about five feet from the stack. The cable angle will add resistance at the top of the movement and the hammer grip offers more emphasis on the brachioradialis muscle."

Burwell's Tip for Dumbbell Curl: "Make sure you maintain a dead hang in your arms with your elbows pointed at the ground throughout. At the top, hold the contraction for two seconds."

Burwell's Tip for TRX Curl: "Your upper arm should be perpendicular to your torso, and there should be a 90-degree angle at your armpit."

HOW TO: FIGURE-8 4-KETTLEBELL FARMER'S WALK

Place two five-pound plates on the floor about 15 feet apart. Select two heavy kettlebells (32-50 kg) and two lighter ones (8 kg is ideal). Hold one light and one heavy kettlebell in each hand and walk in a figure-8 pattern around the five-pound plates. Do 10 laps total. If you can do more than 10 laps with relative ease, use heavier kettle bells.

Optimized Nutrition Volume, 3: building big biceps

SECTION 3: TRICEPS

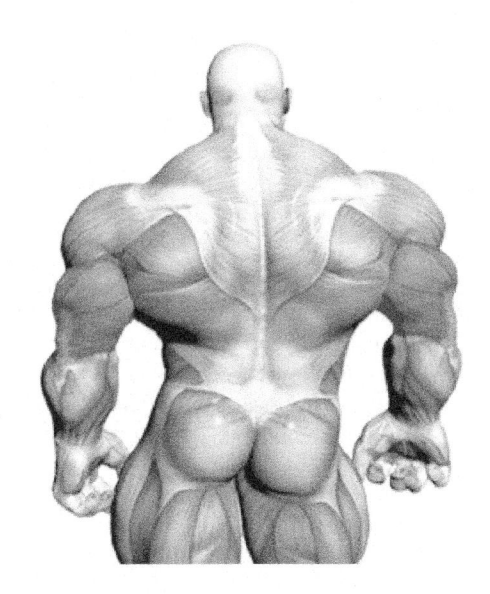

Build Your Upper Arms With the Lying Triceps Extension

Lying triceps extensions have always been among the premier **exercises for filling out your upper arms**, but you may not be getting the full effect. Pointing your guns perpendicular to the floor when you lock the weight out gives your triceps a break—the load transfers to your elbow joints. It's just like the top position of a bench press, and it doesn't **stimulate the triceps**.

Instead, move your arms back a bit so they're about 45 degrees to the floor. When you bend your elbows, the weight will come down below the back of your head, giving the triceps a greater stretch. When you extend your elbows, you can still lock out the weight, giving you the benefit of training through a full range of motion, but your tri's will stay engaged because your arms are at an angle rather than vertical. The pull of gravity will focus the load squarely on the triceps.

Another Advantage - Because the weight never sits directly on the joints, this extension won't aggravate your elbows.

Your 3 Biggest Triceps Training Problems, Solved

Somewhere in the late 80s, a late-night infomercial turned the world of arm-training on its ear. "Triceps represent three quarters of your upper arm mass," the announcer said, matter-of-factly. *Wait, what? Really? Then why the hell do I wreck my biceps all day?*

Now, don't get us wrong, some people out there have understood this for decades but some of us were still slow to catch on. And looking around the gym today, some people are still pretty one-sided with their arm training. To bring balance, symmetry and aesthetics to your arms—if you're into that sort of thing—you need to understand that can't live by curls alone. You need to figure out how to **train your triceps**, especially if you expect to tap into that "three quarters" that infomercial mentions.

Here we address three of the most common complaints we hear from you about **building bigger triceps**, and some practical remedies you can implement today.

1. My biceps tend to overpower my triceps. Why is that and what can I do to fix it?

"Ahhh, the 'show me' muscles!" says New York-based trainer Rocco Castellano, NASM-CPT. "We only work the muscles we can see. You're obviously not hitting your triceps as hard as your biceps. Triceps are three muscles compared to two muscles, so they need to be hit at least one third harder than their counterpart. If you schedule an all-arms day, I would hit your triceps first with two compound movements and one single-joint or finishing movement. On a push day (chest, shoulders, triceps) keep it to two movements, one compound one single-joint move compared to your biceps, which I would limit to one exercise until you feel there is a balance."

"Are you training your biceps alone or with something else like back? What about your triceps? If you're training your biceps alone, then tossing your triceps in at the end of a chest or shoulder workout, you're treating them as an afterthought and that's how they'll respond. And if you're training bi's and tri's together, you probably train biceps first. Try to mix up which muscle group you train first to ensure balance. Finally, don't always chase a pump with your arms—if you expect them to grow, then you need to challenge them with heavier weights in the 8-12-rep range."

2. I just can't seem to bring up that outer horseshoe part of my triceps, even though my inner triceps are pretty meaty.

Castellano, who advocates variety in the gym, suggests shaking things up for getting untapped muscles involved. "Creating a little chaos in the joint does the trick here. You can do that by utilizing cables, ropes and towels on a push down machine. As you push down on the positive phase of the movement you will find that your arms shake a little, this is the instability that I'm talking about. Your neurotransmitters are now asking your brain to recruit another muscle to help out with the load. That's where the weaker heads come in to stabilize the joint."

"Well in any triceps exercise, you're working all three heads of the triceps, just to varying degrees," says Pena. "If your outer, or lateral, head is lagging, you may be doing a few too many skull crushers or overhead dumbbell extensions which hit the long head. Press downs, where your elbows remain at your sides, blast that lateral head."

3. I do plenty of extensions—lying, cables, dumbbells, overhead, kickbacks—but can't seem to add any real size to my tri's. Am I doing something wrong?

"You're doing wussy exercises and you'll stay in Punyville until you step up and complete some heavy compound movements," says an animated Castellano. "Compound movements multiple joints to complete a specific task. Try weighted dips. Another of my favorites is the negative close-grip bench press with a drop. Aim for 3-4 heavy negatives and immediately strip the bar by 30% and perform 15 more reps. Add the weight and start all over for at least two more sets. If you want to get massive you need to push weight, not a hard concept to grasp. Train smart, train hard and get huge."

Pena, who also advocates weighted dips and close-grip benches, suggests trying reverse-grip bench presses with a slightly narrower grip than usual. "These fry your triceps and doing them on a Smith machine allows you to safely overload them without fear of injury."

Target Your Tris With the Triceps Kickback
Hit all three heads of the triceps muscle with

Quick Tips

WHERE IT HITS
Triceps, all three heads (long, lateral, medial)

WHEN TO DO IT
Late in your triceps workout; it makes for a great finishing move.

HOW TO DO IT
3–4 sets, 12–15 reps

this simple muscle-building move.

The three headed triceps brachii is a small muscle, at least when compared with the pecs and back. Yet very few **triceps exercises** actually hit all three heads (long, lateral, and medial) sufficiently. You might think accomplishing this requires a big move with big weights—perhaps a **close-grip bench press** or skull crusher. But one of the best exercises for torching all three triceps heads is actually the kickback. Most guys see it as a shaping move reserved for women. Well, it's also good for mass, and it's time to add it to your routine.

Armed and Ready

Read below for huge kickbacks on your triceps development.

Set Up

1. Hold a dumbbell in one hand with the same side foot on the floor and your opposite knee and hand on a flat bench.
2. Bend over at the waist so your torso is parallel with the floor.
3. Begin with your working arm bent at roughly 90 degrees, your upper arm parallel with the floor, palm facing in, and your elbow in tight against your body.

Do It

Keeping your upper arm stationary, contract your triceps to extend your elbow. Squeeze at the top with your elbow locked out.

Weider Principles: Forced Reps

What It Is

This is one of the best training techniques for getting bigger and stronger—provided it's not overused. Forced reps involve having a spotter assist you in finishing a set, helping you get one or a few extra reps when you're unable to do any more on your own.

What It Does

It allows you to extend a set past initial muscle failure so that the muscle adapts and is eventually able to complete those reps on its own. It's almost like tricking your body into thinking it can do 10 reps when it can do only eight. Before long, you'll actually be doing 10 reps with that same weight.

How to Use It

We advise you to use forced reps on no more than one to two sets per body part in a given workout—more than that and you're asking to be overtrained. On chest, for example, do forced reps on your last set or two of bench press, then cut yourself off from the technique on subsequent pec moves.

5 Ways to Boost Triceps Growth
Add these five methods into your arm routine to start swelling your tris.

The man who wants **bigger triceps** cannot live on pressdowns alone. Too often, we see guys in the gym—and maybe you're one of them—working his triceps to death at the cable pressdown station. Ten sets, 15 sets... whatever it takes to get them sore. But what the pressdown-happy masses don't seem to realize is that this exercise emphasizes the lateral (outer) head of the triceps. So if that's all you do, the other two heads of your tri's are going to be underdeveloped and you'll never get the kind of growth you're hoping for.

There are other versions of this favorite you can use, plus a few exercises and techniques that you are probably neglecting, that will help your cause. Here, you'll find a comprehensive plan—boiled down into five tips—that can help you **build balanced, thick triceps** in no-time flat.

1. Push It

If you must do pressdowns, at least do them properly. Too many guys hold the bar like motorcycle handlebars. This causes you to push with the fingers, which not only places stress on the hands and wrist (as the wrists often extend back), but it reduced the amount of force you can apply to the bar. The key is to push with the heel of the palms. You'll know when you have this technique down as you won't even have to wrap your fingers around the bar. You'll also realize how much more weight you can do on pressdowns. And greater overload equals—you've got it—more triceps growth.

2. Pull It

The flipside to the above advice is to literally do just that—flip your grip and take an underhand grip to pull the weight down when doing triceps pressdowns. While the overhand version places the greatest stress on the lateral triceps head, the underhand version better stresses the oft-neglected medial head. Since the only way to maximize overall triceps mass is to maximize the mass of all three triceps heads, you need to devote time to the medial head as well. Try the reverse-grip pressdown using an EZ-bar attachment with a rotating collar, which will remove the stress form your wrists.

3. Angle It

Every guy that's put in any effort to build up his tri's is familiar with the lying triceps extension, or what is known to hardcore bodybuilders as skullcrushers. We'll bet our crazy magazine salary that you grab the bar and head over to the flat bench. But when's the last time you did them on an incline, or (even crazier) on a decline? Changing the angle of this effective exercise effectively changes the triceps head that's stressed.

The more the arms are placed in front of the body and overhead, the more the long head is emphasized. When you do skullcrushers on a flat bench, the arms are perpendicular to the body and so both the long head and lateral head are fairly equally involved, with even a good bit of involvement from the medial head. When you do them on an incline bench, the arms move more overhead, which places greater emphasis on the long head. And when you do them on a decline bench, the arms move down more towards the sides of the body, similar to a triceps pressdown. This places more stress on the lateral head than the long head, with some help from the medial head at the top of the rep.

4. Band It

You may know that using bands or chains is a great way to increase muscle strength and power due to what is known as linear variable resistance, which means the resistance increases as does the range of motion of the exercise. So why not put them to work in your quest for bigger triceps? Using bands or chains on the close-grip bench press is a fantastic way to maximize triceps involvement.

Since the close-grip bench press is a multi-joint exercise, you are able to maximize the amount of stress you place on the triceps (more weight = more growth). When you press the bar off your chest during the close-grip bench press the triceps involvement increases the higher the bar moves. Since bands and chains increase the resistance as the range of motion increases, using them on the close-grip bench press places maximal stress on the triceps, while minimizing the stress son the chest and delts, which are used in the lower half of the range of motion.

5. Drop It

The Weider Principle known as drop sets is an intensity technique that can be applied to any of the exercises above to push your triceps growth beyond that possible with straight sets. To do a drop set, you simply take a set to failure and then immediately reduce the weight and continue the set to failure again. This can be done one, two, three, or as many times as you want to punish your triceps.

Research performed by our own Weider Research Group discovered that the optimal weight to drop on each drop set is 20—30% of the original weight. We suggest you only do drop sets on the last set or two of each exercise to prevent overtraining. Drop sets work to boost muscle growth by taking the muscle to the point beyond muscle failure. This can help to increase growth hormone release, which stimulates muscle growth.

45-Degree Lying Triceps Extension
With just a slight change in angle, a tried-and-true exercise gets better at helping you build great-looking arms.

ItÂ's fascinating how important angles are to the world around us. For instance, to build a bridge, engineers use a calculated design with many precise angles to ensure the structure strength. Various bridges have multiple angles, making each one distinct for its needs. Angles can also have a huge influence on your workouts. With the traditional lying triceps extension, you begin with your arms extended and the bar directly above your upper chest. In this variation, you All start and finish with your arms at a 45-degree angle Â— a slight change that can bridge the gap between mediocre improvements and phenomenal gains. Follow these steps and get it right.

START
\>> Lie face up on a flat bench with your feet flat on the floor or safely on the bench.
\>> Have a spotter hand you a barbell, and make sure you have a secure, shoulder-width grip on it before he completely releases the bar.
\>> Wrap your thumbs around the bar for safety as you hold it above you.
\>> With your arms straight, allow the bar to slowly travel over your face toward the end of the bench. Stop when your arms reach a 45-degree angle to the bench; this is your starting position.

ACTION
\>> Keeping your upper arms fixed in the start position, bend your elbows to bring the bar down toward the top of your head.
\>> When the bar comes to within an inch or so of the top of your head, pause and hold briefly before pressing the bar back to the top position. Squeeze your triceps at the top and repeat for reps.

POINTERS
\>> If you Are accustomed to the standard version, you All naturally want to bring the bar directly over your body at the start of each rep, both out of habit and for needed rest Â— you All soon realize that this version keeps continuous tension on your triceps at the top. For maximum benefit, try to keep your upper arms in the same angled position throughout each rep. Lighten the weight until you feel completely comfortable and able to perform the exercise properly.
\>> While this version changes the angle of the movement, keeping your elbows in (not allowing them to flare out) is still important for maximizing the exercise benefits.
\>> If you feel discomfort in your elbows or wrists during this exercise, use an EZ-bar instead.
\>> This variation can also be done using dumbbells and a neutral grip. In addition, you can perform this exercise one arm at a time, which allows you to use your opposite arm as a means to spot yourself in case you donÂ't have a partner to assist you.

7 Ways to Torch Your Tri's

Triceps account for roughly two-thirds of your upper arm mass. So why in the name of Arnold do you spend so much more time blasting your biceps? If your true aim is to start using more tape measure around your arms, then you're going to need to **attack your tri's** with greater intensity. And once you've made that commitment, it's time to refine your strategy.

Our expert panel offers its collective wisdom on coaxing the most growth out of this muscle group. But you can forget about hearing another cozy prescription for a few extra sets of pressdowns – these guys are going to help you **push your triceps** to their breaking point so you can get the bulbous, sickly-striated finish that you've always wanted.

1. DOWN SHIFT

Have you ever seen John Cena's triceps? Well, if you haven't, "tiny" is not a word that would be used to describe them. And though Cena is one of the hardest working men in show biz, he's taken a fair share of his cues from WWE coach Rob MacIntyre, CSCS. When it comes to triceps specifically, MacIntyre likes to have his clients slow things down a bit.

"I like to use slow reps when training triceps especially on the eccentric portion of the lift," he says. "Most of the time, the athletes I work with are training triceps explosively as part of other movements. However, when it is time to be pretty and get the big guns, I like to slow the reps down for isolations exercises. It is easy to develop tendonitis by trying to use fast, explosive heavy movements during isolation work due to the stress on the elbow joint. A triceps extension with a 5-10 second eccentric phase changes the game in terms of getting a pump. If you're new to this type of training, be careful as the triceps tend to give out suddenly."

>> TRI THIS: Lead off your triceps routine with 3-4 sets of triceps pressdowns or skullcrushers. Select a weight you'd use for 10-12 reps but use a 5-10 second negative on each rep – followed by an explosive concentric, or positive lift – and shoot for eight solid reps.

2. GET MECHANICAL

"One of my favorite triceps tactics involves using mechanical advantage on the close-grip bench press with boards," he says. "To do this, complete five, full range of motion close grip bench presses. Don't rack the weight. Hold the bar pressed out at full extension. Next, have your spotter place one board lengthwise on your torso, so that the board runs from your belly to the middle of your chest. Repeat the exercise for another five reps, lowering the barbell until it touches the board. After each five reps, your partner will add one board to the stack. Little by little, this shortens your range of motion, working your triceps in different ways until you finish with four boards stacked on your chest. That's 25 reps. It's also just one set." Bryant likes using this tactic because, he says, it combines aspects of rest-pause training, partial reps, cheating and drop sets.

3. FINISH WITH FAILURE

If your routine already consists of a challenging battery of close-grip bench presses, dips and skull crushers, you're on the right track. But how you finish is just as important as how you start. David Sandler, MS, CSCS, believes in getting a skin-stretching pump because of its effect on protein synthesis (read: it increases it).

"I love hitting the triceps pressdown at the end of the routine and doing drops on each set and finishing with some close-grip push-ups," he says. "I try to hit eight reps on the pressdown set working at max, then the I drop about 25 percent and continue until I cannot get another full rep on my own. Immediately after, I drop to the ground, keep my hands no wider than shoulder-width, and bang out as many pushups as possible. I give myself a generous 90-second rest and do the whole thing again for a second and then third set. Your tri's get so jacked with a pump, when you leave the gym, everyone knows it."

4. DROP IT

"By far, my favorite intensity technique when training triceps is using a drop set on the last set of *each* triceps exercise to really stimulate muscle growth," he says. "To do this simply drop the weight down approximately 25-30 percent from your original weight for as many reps as you can handle. If you're doing it right, the tri's should be screaming at you! Drop sets take the muscle to the point beyond muscle failure thus yielding some serious results in your overall upper arm development."

5. VOLUMIZE

Why do 10 reps when 20 will do? This is a favorite refrain of the high-volume training crowd, which believes that muscles thrive on high-rep, high-set challenges. Justin Grinnell, CSCS, isn't so single-minded in his approach but thinks that "more is better" is a philosophy that your triceps can benefit from.

"My favorite training intensity technique for triceps are high-rep supersets," he says. "Since the triceps get a ton of heavy work from overhead presses, dips and bench presses, I like to get as much blood into the muscle as possible with isolation movements done back-to-back. Doing this will tap into some other muscle fibers that were not hit during the heavy work. I like lying dumbbell triceps extensions superset with overhead rope extensions for four sets of 15 reps. Make sure to keep continuous tension – don't pause at the bottom of any rep. You want to force as much blood into the muscle as possible, and create as much time under tension as possible to maximize muscle tissue breakdown."

6. HIT SOME POSES (…SERIOUSLY)

One thing missing from most triceps routines is a focus on achieving a peak contraction – a deliberate, powerful pause at the top of every rep. But with the triceps, this is an especially valuable tool – since the primary job of the triceps is to extend the elbow, achieving and holding that extension can boost positional strength while also summoning more muscle fibers into play. M&F advisory board member Eric the Trainer knows this and prefers to take advantage of it, in unconventional but highly beneficial fashion. He just wants you to flex.

"Using an engorging, or flexing, phase directly following each set with a 10-second hold can blood to the region, supercharging the desired results," he says.

7. STEP UP YOUR SELECTION

Attention: back away from the cable station! Too many of us have grown averse to the idea of truly testing ourselves when it comes to building a better physique. But, as Phil Gephart, MS, CSCS, that is exactly why proven, meat-and-potatoes training is superior to fancy techniques any day of the week.

"When we are talking intensity we're not talking 'let's sweat a lot and work really hard and really fast' but rather intensity from a training standpoint is simply a number relative to your one rep max," he says. "So when we go in an intensification phase we are raising the load or using heavier weight. For training triceps during an intensification phase, I feel the most bang for your buck would be to incorporate dips. But you have to make sure you use a full range of motion where the bicep touches the forearm at the bottom of the ROM and your elbows are 99% straight at the top. Because we are talking intensification, shoot for around six repetitions. What that means for most of you guys is that you will probably need to add a weight belt or some apparatus were you can hang weight from your body. Remember, when looking to do six repetitions we want that to be the last rep you could possibly do with *maybe* one more in reserve. So if you could do 8-10 (or more) it simply isn't heavy enough. Add some more weight, meat."

HORSESHOE FEEDER

Combine these supplements when trying to add size to your tri's.

Supplement Dose/Timing

Whey Protein 20 g pre-workout, 20-40 g post-workout

Casein Protein 10-20 g post-workout

BCAA 5-10 g pre- and post-workout

Creatine 2-5 g pre- and post-workout

Beta Alanine 2-3 g pre- and post-workout

Optimized Nutrition Volume, 3: building big biceps

Mr. Olympia Phil Heath's Triceps Routine

The reigning Mr. Olympia's triceps may be otherworldly, but his triceps routine is grounded to reality.

Reigning Mr. Olympia Phil Heath never had to worry about his triceps. "It's not that I don't want big triceps, but the truth is, I've never had much difficulty adding mass to them," he once stated. Lucky bastard.

Still, Heath knew early in his bodybuilding career that if he wanted to become the world's greatest bodybuilder, he couldn't rest on his horseshoe-shaped laurels. Instead of just relying on the genetic gifts he had, he hammered away at those horseshoes, and in time forged what are now among the greatest triceps the world has ever seen.

While Heath relies on tried-and-true triceps-building exercises, he likes to mix things up by incorporating the Fascia Stretch Training technique (aka FST-7), devised by his trainer, Hany Rambod. FST-7 involves finishing off a body part with seven sets of an exercise performed for 6–8 reps and with 30-45 seconds of rest between sets.

Excercise	Sets	Reps
One-arm Dumbbell Extensions	3	10-12
Two-arm Dumbbell Kickbacks	3	10-12
Weighted Dips	2	10-12
Cable Pushdowns*	7	8-12

Add More Size to Your Tris
Try these highly effective moves to build a bigger pair of sweeping triceps.

You know what makes a truly impressive arm? One that can simply hang down…unflexed…and still look as if it belongs on a gorilla, rather than on a human. That look does not come about from having huge biceps, but from having thick. More specifically, it comes from a highly developed inner (or long) triceps head. This is the head of the triceps responsible for that "sweep" under the biceps in a front biceps pose, and the dramatic thickness on the back of the upper arm seen in a back lat-spread pose.

Ok, so what is required to achieve a pair of "sweeping" triceps? Intelligent, targeted training. Just like it takes specific movements to force more brachialis than biceps recruitment, it takes certain types of **triceps exercises** to get more inner head activation.

Key to Building Sweeping Triceps

The key lies in choosing exercises that force the elbows up by the ears throughout the movement. EMG studies have shown that this is the optimal arm positioning to utilize when looking for the strongest activation of inner (long) triceps head fibers.

On the next page are three of the most effective "sweep-producing" triceps movements around, and how to perform them.

1. Incline Overhead Barbell Extension

Lie down on an incline bench set at about 60 degrees. Make sure you're up high enough on the bench so that your head is just off the top. Have someone hand you a straight or EZ curl bar, and grip just inside shoulder width.

Point your elbows up toward the ceiling and keep them locked in that position throughout your set. Lower the bar slowly back behind your head and allow for a deep stretch of the triceps.

As you bring the bar back up, do not allow elbows to creep forward or you will rob your triceps of major growth stimulation. Lock the arms out straight by intensely contracting the triceps, not by hyper extending at the elbows.

2. Seated Single Arm Overhead Dumbbell Extension

Sit on a bench that has support and does not extend past your upper back. Grab a dumbbell in such a way that the meat of your hand by your pinkie finger is right up against the plates. Hold the dumbbell overhead with your palm facing almost completely to the front. Make sure the elbow is pointing straight toward the ceiling and lock it there.

Slowly lower the dumbbell behind your head, but keep the palm facing almost forward, so that the bell angles toward the opposite ear as it descends.

The exact angle that you are able to use during the eccentric contraction will depend largely on your shoulder flexibility. Make sure to get a full stretch at the bottom before using pure triceps power to re-straighten the arm.

Heavy weight can be used in the exercise, but never use a weight so heavy that it turns into a half-press. This is a very common training mistake that will rob you of much of the benefit of this movement.

3. Cable Overhead Extensions Using Rope Attachment

Attach a rope to an upper pulley at a cable crossover station. Grab the ends of the rope while facing away from the weight stack. Bring one leg forward until you are in a lunge-like position, and lean over until your torso is about parallel to the floor. Your elbows should be right up by your ears and they should remain there throughout the set.

Starting from the stretched position, use pure triceps strength to begin to straighten the arms. However, as you are doing so, turn the palms from their initial position (facing the head) to a downward position (facing the floor). This will cause the ends of the rope to spread away from each other and allow for a very powerful "cramping" of the triceps. Squeeze hard at the peak contraction point, and then reverse the movement into a full stretch once again.

As strength begins to dwindle it will become increasingly difficult to continue spreading the rope at the top of the movement. When this occurs, simply keep the palms facing, from stretch to contraction and you will find you can get a few extra reps.

Optimized Nutrition Volume, 3: building big biceps

Section 3: Forearms

Build Bigger Forearms Now
Focus on this neglected muscle to construct forearms Popeye would envy.

The muscle you're referring to is called the brachioradialis. It starts on the upper arm bone, crosses the elbow joint, and attaches to the ulna (the large forearm bone). Some genetically fortunate guys can grow their brachioradialis muscles through their back and **biceps workouts** alone. The rest of us need to take a more direct approach to see any real growth.

To place more focus on the brachioradialis and less on the biceps when performing a **barbell curl**, flip your grip from underhand to overhand. Using an overhand grip on an EZ-bar places even more focus on the brachioradialis.

To do the reverse-grip EZ-bar curl, hold an EZ-bar with an overhand grip as shown. To specifically target the brachioradialis, push your elbows back and keep the bar close to your body as you raise it.

The Workout

Excercise	Sets	Reps	Rest
Reverse-Grip EZ-bar Curl	3	8-12	1 min
Barbell Wrist Curl	3	8-12	1 min
Superset w/ Barbell Reverse Wrist Curl	3	8-12	1 min

Quick Tip

Instead of curling the weight in an arc, keep the movement of the bar in more of a vertical (straight up and down) path.

The Ultimate Forearm Routine
Three weeks to bowling-pin-size development in your forearms.

The forearms consist primarily of slow-twitch muscle fibers, which means they're built for endurance and respond best to duration activities, like carrying furniture and holding on for dear life. Employing high volume and short rest periods will inflate your forearms fast.

Directions

Follow this program for three weeks. Perform the workout two to three times per week after training your other body parts. Allow at least a day to recover in between.

Complete the exercises as a circuit, doing a set of A, followed by a set of B, and so on, before resting. Repeat for three total circuits.

Week 1

1A Seated Barbell Wrist Curl
Reps: 12

1B Standing Reverse Wrist Curl w/ EZ-curl Bar
Reps: 12

1C Standing Dumbbell Hammer Curl
Reps: 12

Rest 90 seconds and repeat

Week 2

1A Seated Dumbbell Wrist Curl
Reps: 12

1B Seated Reverse Dumbbell Wrist Curl
Reps: 12

1C Standing Reverse Barbell Curl
Reps: 12

Rest 90 seconds and repeat

Week 3

1A Standing Cable Wrist Curl
Reps: 15
Attach a short straight bar to the low pulley and bend your arms 90 degrees. Do wrist curls from that position.

1B Standing Cable Reverse Curl
Reps: 15
Set up the same as for the above but with palms facing down.

1C Dumbbell Hammer Curl
Reps: 12

Rest 90 seconds and repeat

*Feel free to use grip-enhancing equipment, like **Grip4orce** sleeves or **Fat Gripz**, to make the exercises more challenging and recruit more forearm muscles.

Bigger Forearms & Stronger Shoulders

your questions about how to add size and strength to forearms and how to avoid shoulder damage during military presses.

Question 1: "Would you say reverse barbell curls are the best forearm builder for strength and mass?"

Yes, reverse curls with a barbell are an excellent exercise for building massive forearms while simultaneously growing the biceps—as long as the straight bar does not irritate your wrists or elbows. If this is the case, just use an EZ curl bar as a substitute for the straight bar. Another very good movement is barbell wrist curls performed with your forearms resting on your legs or the bench, with the bar and your hands hanging over.

While it is true you can get a sick grip by incorporating tools like towels and ropes into your training, for exercises like rope rows or towel pull-ups, to get more size, you need more volume. This is because your forearms are predominantly slow-twitch muscle fibers which respond best to high repetition work. So you'll want to get up into the 4 sets of 20 rep range with your reverse curls and wrist curls.

Question 2: "When performing a military seated shoulder press, I am getting a clicking in my left shoulder. How can I prevent this?"

You're probably okay if the clicking sound is not accompanied by pain, but you can also just try a different angle on the bench. Sometimes that is all it takes to get a better setup and prevent issues during the press. I would also ensure that you're always working on improving your posture. If your upper back is tight and your shoulders are rounded forward, your shoulder blades will not be in a good position, which will affect the tracking of your upper arm and strength potential for your press. As a rule, incorporating face pulls with lots of foam rolling on the upper back will always be a good idea for anyone who does a lot of barbell and dumbbell pressing movements.

On the Fores Front
Dedicated training is the only way to build dense, muscular forearms. Try these two routines to boost your grip and jumpstart growth.

What is the best way to **build your forearm**s? Wrist curls and extensions? Well, those are certainly the most popular methods but that's only for a lack of creativity and the sad relegation of forearms to a silent bodypart in the quest for a better physique. It's time to get your forearms growing. And there are far more ways to do it than you might think.

While hang-holding objects for grip is reliable for building a vise-like grip, for size improvement, you need to follow the same basic rules of development that you use for your other muscles: use heavier weight, perform fewer reps and add lots of volume to your program.

Sure you can do the standard wrist curls and extensions with heavy dumbbells or even a few sets of hammer curls. Or, you can do a few extra things and really see your forearms grow. First, check out clubbells. While most gyms do not have them, you can get yourself a couple different sizes and do some hammer extensions and flexions (known as abduction and adduction) as well as pronating and supinating your arm extended out from supports.

If you don't want to buy clubbells, disassemble one side of your dumbbell or grab a short-bar attachment and you are ready to rock.

Another underused method of **building grip** and forearm strength is the **towel pull-up**. Hang a towel over a high bar, grab tight at either end and do your pull-ups.

Another solid forearm incorporator is the fat bar, a standard length barbell that is a little thicker in diameter than the standard 1-inch Olympic barbell. You perform exercises with a fat bar just the same except that the barbell is much harder to hold since your thumb and fingers can't overlap. This forces the wrist flexors to fire on every rep just to keep your grip.

Treat your forearms like you would your biceps and triceps. Hit them hard for 8-12 reps using a challenging weight for 3-4 sets on a variety of exercises.

Exercise	Sets/Reps
Towel pull-ups (weighted)	3/8
Fat-bar curl	3/10
Hammer curl	3/10
4-way clubbell+	3/10

+ A giant set consisting of extension, flexion, adduction and abduction.

Clubbed Mass

If you're tired of gimmicky grip gadgets and are looking for something dynamic and novel to fill out your forearms, you might want to give clubbells a try. These top-heavy, tapered weights allow you to work your grip, wrists and forearms through various planes, making them our fave implement for training this bodypart. They range in size from 5 pounds to 45 pounds, although we recommend using the lighter clubbells (5 or 10 pounds, depending on your level of strength) for your forearm work. They're not the cheapest weights in the world - prices start at $84.95 - but their versatility and durability make it worth the stretch.

The All-Clubbell Forearm Routine

Exercise	Sets/Reps
Cable wrist curl to hold	3/30-60 sec
Weighted supination/pronation	3/10-12
Weighted wrist abduction	3/10-12

Weighted wrist adduction   3/10-12

Around the clock   3/10-12

Clubbell Exercise Descriptions

Cable wrist curl to hold
Stand midway between two weight stacks holding two low-pulley D-handles out to your sides, palms down. Roll the handle as far out into your hands as possible before using your wrists to curl the weight back toward your forearms. Aim for a weight that causes positive muscle failure in the prescribed rep range. After completing the final rep, simply hold the weight in a neutral position for an additional 30-60 seconds - as prescribed - to round out the set.

Wrist supination/pronation
Pick up a short, straight bar attachment or light clubbell and stand holding it at one end, arm bent at a 90-degree angle, your elbow pinned to your side. Starting with the attachment perpendicular to the ceiling and without moving your elbow, slowly rotate your wrist in toward your body (pronation) until the bar is parallel to the ground. Pause for a count and rotate your wrist back the other direction (supination) until the bar is again parallel to the ground. This constitutes one full repetition. Complete the prescribed number of reps before switching arms.

Weighted wrist abduction
Stand holding a short, straight bar attachment or light clubbell at your side, elbow pinned to your ribs, the heavy end of the bar pointed down and nearly perpendicular to the floor in front of you. Bending only at your wrist and keeping the weight in line with your forearm, raise the bar up to a point at or just above parallel to the floor. Pause for a peak contraction and lower it back to the starting position before repeating for reps.

Weighted wrist adduction
Stand holding a short, straight bar attachment or clubbell at your side, elbow pinned to your ribs, the heavy end of the bar pointed down and nearly perpendicular to the floor behind you. Bending only at your wrist and keeping the weight in line with your forearm, raise the bar up to a point at or just above parallel to the floor. Pause for a peak contraction and lower it back to the starting position before repeating for reps.

Around the Clock
Stand holding a short, straight bar attachment or clubbell at your side, elbow pinned to your ribs, the heavy end of the bar pointed down and nearly perpendicular to the floor in front of you. Bending only at your wrist, slowly raise the bar as high as you can, in line with your arm (as with wrist abduction). Making that point 12 o'clock, slowly rotate the weight clockwise as wide as you can on an imaginary clock in front of you. Returning to 12 o'clock constitutes one full rep. Completing all reps in each direction makes up one full set.

Neglected Body Parts: Forearms and Calves
Often overlooked during weight training, these muscles need some love too. So give it to them!

How often do you see people in the gym neglecting certain body parts, or leaving weaker body parts to the end of their workouts and treating them like an afterthought? Two body parts that are most often overlooked are the calves and forearms. Let's take a closer look at how we can give these muscle groups the attention they deserve.

Calves can be one of the hardest body parts to develop and train properly. I know many people who have had lifelong difficulty getting them to grow more than just a couple of inches. However, there are several ways in which lifters can improve this stubborn body part:

Prioritize Calves: Don't Make Them an Afterthought

Most people still treat their calf training as an "extra" at the end of a hard legs workout. Those who really need work on this muscle group must train them hard and heavy with as much focus as any other muscle group.

Some bodybuilders like to work their calves before they train the rest of their legs, but I think this presents a potential to fatigue your legs and hamper your strength on squats. So why not train your calves at the very beginning of an UPPER body workout, so that there is no interference between muscle groups. The best training days for this are ones that might not take as long, such as chest or arms.

here are 3 major muscle groups in the lower leg. If you want to build the calves to their fullest potential, you MUST include calf muscle exercises that work each of the following 3 major muscle groups.

Gastrocnemius

This is the largest calf muscle and the one that most people work. This is the one that you see when flexing and looking down at your calves. Standing calf raise exercises, donkey calf raises, and all variations of those two calf muscle exercises will work the large gastrocnemius muscle. If the leg is not bent and you do a calf raise, the gastrocnemius is being worked.

Soleus

The soleus gives the calves depth and thickness because it lies beneath the larger gastrocnemius muscle. If you looked at someones calves as you were standing behind them, you would see the soleus muscles running down both sides of the lower leg. The soleus is worked during calf muscle exercises in which the knee is bent. So any variation of seated calf raises or squat raises will best work this muscle.

Tibialis Anterior

The tibialis anterior is almost always ignored. It's the huge frontal muscle that you can see if you flex your toe upwards and watch the area below the front part of your knee. This muscle goes all the way down the front part of your lower leg. If you haven't been working your tibialis anterior, you've been missing out. Reverse calf raises of any type will work the tibialis anterior.

he best forearm exercises are compound exercises that allow the use of heavy weights. In addition, a variety of isolation movements are also great for strengthening and building muscle in the forearms. Follow these isolation exercises to work your forearms to the max.

Dumbbell Wrist Curls:

This exercise targets the forearm flexors and allows you to work each forearm individually, thus helping to develop balance and proportion between both forearms.

Sit and hold a dumbbell with an underhand grip. Rest your forearm on the bench between your thighs with your wrist just beyond the edge of the bench.

Allow the dumbbell to roll down the palm towards the fingers. Curl the dumbbell back up and flex your wrist. Once you perform the desired number of reps for one arm, switch and repeat with the other arm.

Barbell Wrist Curl:

This is a basic forearm exercise that works the forearm flexor muscles.

Sit on a flat bench and lay your forearms on your lap while holding a barbell palms up. Using only your hands and wrists, curl the barbell up toward the ceiling as high as possible, keeping your forearms flat on your lap. When you return to the start position, allow the barbell to roll all the way down into your fingertips and then repeat.

Optimized Nutrition Volume, 3: building big biceps

Straight-Up Forearms Workout
Stop neglecting half of your arms. Get thicker forearms and a stronger grip with this brutal routine.

You can see them in gyms, hanging out of sports cars, or perched atop armrests as you walk the aisle of a commercial jetliner. they're the key to possessing an iron grip and a bone-crushing handshake. their size and density help define the masculinity and blue-collar work ethic of a man, yet the forearms are often not directly targeted in many workout regimens. Well, dust off that can of spinach in the back of your kitchen cabinet, because is about to inject some serious forearm action into your program and bring out your inner Popeye.

The Routine

The **forearms** serve a number of duties. Not only do they flex and extend the wrists, but perhaps more important, they contract statically (along with the muscles of the hands) to assist in gripping heavy objects. It's easy to see, then, how a weak pair of forearms could be the limiting factor in possessing elite-level strength. They also round out a top-level physique. If your grip is lacking, so too will be the amount of weight you can use on deadlifts, rows, weighted pullups, and other measures of brute strength. Guess how many successful **strongman** competitors have a weak grip: zero. Same goes for the top competitors in the IFBB—you got 'em or you can't win.

The following workout addresses all of the aforementioned duties. Wrist flexion and extension is covered in the first two exercises with curling motions, as is the brachiolradialis muscle, which sits up close to the elbow, via reverse curls. Plate pinch holds are an isometric exercise designed to provide grip strength that will carry over to other gym exercises as well as athletic activities. The finisher is a traditional wrist roller that involves continuous wrist extension with a front deltoid isometric hold.

Exercise	Sets	Reps

Optimized Nutrition Volume, 3: building big biceps

Barbell Wrist Curl	3	12
Barbell Reverse Curl + Reverse Wrist Curl	3	10-15
Plate Pinch Hold	3	20-30 seconds
Wrist Roller	2	Full Length of Chain*

* Up and down

The Basics

→Insert this forearm routine at the end of any regularly scheduled workout, or do it on its own on an off day.

→ Keep rest periods brief during the workout—60 seconds max between sets. the routine shouldn't take more than around 15 minutes to complete.

Barbell Wrist Curl

Sit in the middle of a flat bench with your legs straddling it and hold a barbell with your hands about six inches apart, palms facing up and using a thumbless (monkey) grip. Bend over at the waist and place the backs of your forearms against the bench with your hands and wrists over the edge. Begin with your wrists extended so that your hands are below your forearms. Keeping your arms stationary, flex your wrists as far as possible to lift the bar up in a relatively short range of motion. Squeeze your forearms for a full second, then return to the start position, lowering the bar until you feel a full stretch.

Tips

- Keep the elbows close together by pushing in with your legs so that your arms can't spread apart during the set.
- Increase weight on every set. Feel free to utilize the fixed weight barbell rack so you don't have to change plates between sets.

Barbell Reverse Curl + Reverse Wrist Curl

Stand holding a barbell in front of your body with a thumbless, reverse grip (palms facing behind you) and your arms hanging straight down toward the floor. Slowly curl the bar up, keeping your elbows in close to the body. At the top of the movement, flex the wrists back fully, then slowly lower the barbell along the same path you lifted it up, curling the wrists under at the bottom of the movement.

Tips

- If a straight bar bothers your wrists, feel free to use an EZ-curl bar instead.
- Don't lean back as you curl the bar up; keep your torso perpendicular with the floor. If you have to, perform this exercise standing in front of a wall or other solid structure to keep you upright.

Plate Pinch Hold

Find two plates of the same weight—if you're new to this exercise, start with two 5- or 10-pound plates and work your way up from there. From a standing position, squeeze the two plates together at your side (arm extended toward the floor) in one hand. Do this for 20–30 seconds and then switch hands and repeat. Use a heavier pair of plates on each set, as long as you can hold them together for at least 20 seconds. if and when holding two 45s becomes easy for 30 seconds, increase the set duration to 45–60 seconds.

Tips

- With traditional plates, where one side is flat and the other is hollowed out, keep the flat sides together.
- Choose weights that are challenging and keep your feet clear of slipping plates.

Wrist Roller

Secure a weight plate to the end of the chain or cord of a wrist roller. Stand holding the bar of the wrist roller out in front of you with a shoulder-width grip, arms extended parallel to the floor and the chain fully unwound so the plate is in the bottom-most position. Alternately extend your wrists to rotate the bar and wrap the chain around it so the plate inches upward. When the plate reaches the bar, reverse the motion under control to lower the weight back down.

- On the way up, you can twist the chain quickly, but don't let it down fast—much of this exercise's benefit is derived from the eccentric motion. Going too fast will eliminate the effect.
- You'll be focusing on initiating the movement with the forearms, but this exercise also taxes the front deltoids and can be an excellent core challenge, too.

Strengthen Your Grip for Bigger Forearms

Make like a strongman and crush the competition with some direct forearm work.

The Setup

In his classic *Encyclopedia of Modern Bodybuilding*, Arnold Schwarzenegger warned you not to use straps for your **pulling exercise**s. But you've been wearing them for years anyway and now your forearm and grip size and strength are lagging behind, just like Arnold said they would. It's time for some dedicated forearm training to make up the difference and pay homage to the Austrian Oak. With this circuit, along with some simple and inexpensive grip tools you can make – and use – at home, you too can look like you work for a living, even if you don't.

The Solution

When it comes to grip strength, you need to develop three separate but equally important abilities. First, you need to be able to grab things and hold onto them. Next, you need to be able to grab things and crush them. Finally, you need to be able to pinch things between your thumb and fingers – your "pincer" grip – and both hold onto them and crush them. Whether you want to develop size in your forearms or "grab cloth and hang on" when making a tackle in football, strengthening all three of these qualities will serve you well.

To **strengthen your crushing grip**, use a wrist roller and a good gripper – the steel ones strongmen competitors use, not the ones you'll find at your local sporting goods store. For your holds, use a fat bar. If your gym doesn't have one, fold two towels to an identical width and wrap them around a barbell so it's thick enough to be difficult to hang onto in a standing position without touching it to your body. For your pincer grip, start with 15-20-pound hex dumbbells held for time, and work your way up. To perform, place the dumbbells on the floor vertically and pick them up by the head and hold.

You'll either need to purchase a wrist roller – most gyms don't have them – or make your own. To do this, have your local hardware store cut a 16" length of 1½" PVC pipe. Bore a hole through the middle, tie a knot in a piece of cord and string it through. Attach a carabiner to the end of the cord and you've got yourself the best forearm developer on the market for under $5. When performing the actual exercise, lean your forearms on something at chest height – one spotter bar of a power rack is perfect for this purpose – so your shoulder strength doesn't become a limiting factor.

The Workout

Exercise	Sets	Reps	Rest
Fat Bar Hold	2	Max Time	90 sec
Hex Dumbbell Hold	2	Max Time	90 sec
Grippers	3	To Failure	60 sec
Supported Wrist Roller	2	Up/Down	90 sec

The Lift Doctor: Bigger Forearms & Less Back Soreness

Follow this prescription for how to boost forearm size & reduce back stiffness.

"What's the best way to boost your forearms to a bigger size?" –

I've written about **how to get bigger forearms** before but let's dive deeper into the training. As I stated, you need to smash forearms with lots and lots of volume. Also, they should typically be done after your arm work, because training your biceps and triceps first, will act to *pre-exhaust* to your forearms. And, you don't want to have trouble holding onto the weights, which will happen if you hit forearms first in the workout.

Some of my favorite forearms exercises are barbell wrist curls with the bar on the edge of the bench and seated wrist curls with the bar under your legs as you sit off the edge of the bench. Two other favorites are EZ curl bar reverse curls and reverse wrist curls. These four simple exercises will add mass on your forearms like no others.

Strengthening the forearms in another matter. Having a strong grip is the definition of being a man and affects everything we do in the gym. If we can grip the weights tighter, we will be stronger and more stabile for whatever exercise we do. While there are a ton of grip strengthening exercises to choose from, I've found the more *dynamic* the movement, the greater carry over to your absolute grip strength. Exercises like high-rep Kettlebell swings, heavy side rows without straps, heavy barbell shrugs, rack holds (where you hit a rack pull off the cage and hold the weight as long as you can), and farmer's walk variations; will turn your grip into a vise.

After a heavy back day, what are the best stretches to fight off soreness?

Recent research (Henschke, 2011) has shown that stretching, in fact, doesn't really help with delayed onset of muscle soreness or DOMS; as much as we had previously thought. It still will crush you the next day and then hit the peak soreness around two days after that heavy workout – no matter how much you stretch afterwards.

With that being said, stretching as part of your comprehensive fitness program is really important to help you overcome another negative effect of training; restricted movement. As you recover and your muscles repair themselves, they shorten. Your movement becomes limited. Keeping your movement, especially as you get older, will make the difference between leading a fit life, or walking around with a cane.

Light activity, stretching, and mobility after a heavy session will keep your mobile, agile and hostile. These activities can be done in between your normal workouts in an extra 15-20 minute session. These "extra sessions" should include foam rolling, shoulder recovery work with a band, stretching, dynamic mobility, and **breathing drills**. You will recover fast and feel great. Being better recovered will also allow you to train harder when your next workout rolls around.

Below are two great routines; one to target the upper back and shoulders and one to open up the hips:

Awesome 3-Minute Shoulder Warm-up with a Band

Bust Out Bigger Forearms

Give these moves a try to add circumference and strength to your lower arms.

Your **strong, powerful forearms** are your infantry. They're your grunts. In the U.S. Army and Marines, "GRUNT" stood for General, Replacement, Untrained. We're going to turn that last part into "UNTamable!"

I want you to do four sets of each of the movements below, back to back, no rest, switching up the order each time you do them. You'll finish with three consecutive timed holds (hanging from a pull-up bar) with your rest period being double the time of your hang (i.e., if you hang for 42 seconds, rest for 1 minute 24 seconds, then hang again, and so on).

The Exercises

Here are your movements: wrist curls, wrist extensions, handshake curls (bending your thumb toward your forearm and back) using a dumbbell, and squeeze (Captains of Crush have a terrific selection of hand grippers that can sit on your desk).

For all four moves, start with a weight that stops you in your tracks at 10–12 reps for the first set, 15–20 the second, 20–25 the third, and 25-plus for the final set. You may want to have a friend drive you home after one week of this.

Big Forearms, Crushing Grip

Here's what you need to know...

- There's no sport that isn't benefitted by stronger hands, especially sports where holding a piece of equipment is required.

- Bodybuilders are often only concerned with forearm size, which requires an entirely different approach from grip strength.

- For a stronger grip, choose passive crushing, active crushing, pinch gripping, and thick bar work.

- For bigger forearms, choose wrist curling, static holds, and extensor work, all with moderate loads for higher reps.

Big, intimidating forearms are a sign of power. No one picks a fight with the guy who sports mitts that look like they could uncork a fire hydrant. But are you chasing grip strength or forearm size? Let's talk about how to train for both.

Pick a Primary Goal: Grip Strength or Big Forearms?

If you're concerned with grip strength, it's probably sport or powerlifting related. Implemental sports (especially those that use an implement like a bat, club, or stick) are greatly improved when the athlete's hands are strong and dexterous. Martial arts, rock climbing, and gymnastics all require tons of maximal gripping. The fact is, there's really no sport that isn't benefitted by stronger hands.

At the gym, pulling heavy weight requires holding heavy weight, and wrist strength is required to stabilize a heavy bench press. Weak wrists can't push heavy loads.

That said, some iron warriors are merely concerned with forearm size, which is okay as having big forearms is an impressive, dominant characteristic both on the stage and street.

Considering those are very different goals, you need to make sure the training is specific. Think of it like powerlifting versus bodybuilding – different goals with different training methods.

Let's discuss the elements of a sensible grip program for the typical lifter.

Chasing Maximal Grip Strength

implements You Should Own
Open-hand (thick) implement: Fat Gripz/Tyler Grips/Grip4orce/Grenade balls/rock rings

Spend $40 on any one of the grip tools out there and make use of it. They'll fit in the gym bag and pay for themselves when you tear the popped collar off some ornery frat boy's polo shirt.

Spring-loaded grippers of 150 and 200-pound closing force. Captains of Crush, Heavy Grippers, whatever – they all work. We personally use Captains of Crush and most of our 17-22 year-olds use the 1.5 and 2.0.

Elements Of A Good Program

Passive Crushing
Holding a crushing-grip where gravity is forcing the hand to open, such as you'd experience in holding a heavy dumbbell or barbell. This implement (dumbbell, barbell, or kettlebell) provides resistance by way of gravity.

Active Crushing
Active crushing involves squeezing something that resists the hand from closing, such as a spring-loaded gripper. Understand you may not be that strong in active crushing, even if you can hold 500-plus pounds in your hands. The act of getting the hand closed under resistance, which passive gripping doesn't provide, is often overlooked.

Pinch Gripping
Pinch gripping involves squeezing the extended fingers towards the thumb without flexing individual digits, such as you'd experience holding a textbook.

Open-Hand
An open-hand grip involves passively holding an object that's so large the fingers and thumb can't overlap. Fat Gripz and fat bars are examples of open-hand held implements.

Lower Reps and Hold Durations
Maximal strength requires maximal holds, which I'll define as four reps or less, or 10 seconds or less of a static hold.

If you combine these elements in a solid mix, you'll be on your way to having an exceptional grip. Note that all these actions attempt to close the hand, which involves only the muscles of the anterior compartment of the forearm. i.e., the flexor/proctors. Maintaining healthy forearms and hands will need balance, which we'll address later.

Chasing Maximal Forearm Size

Implements You Should Own
Wrist Roller

Buy one if you want, but a homemade version of PVC pipe (1.5-2 inches is perfect) with climbing webbing attached is a cheap and amazing solution. You can pack a shortie that can attach to a cable machine, or a longer power-rack version that you'll fall in love with.

Check our versions below that we made out of aluminum tubing. The beauty of sitting them in a rack or attaching to a cable column is that you can truly test the grip without the shoulders giving out first.

Open-hand (thick) implement: Fat Gripz/Tyler Grips/Grip4orce/Grenade balls/rock rings

Elements Of A Good Program

Wrist Curling
To develop that big flexor/pronator belly, you need to use wrist flexion. Really heavy wrist curls bother a lot of my clients' wrists, so we usually go for sets of 8-plus and seek a pump rather than maximal strength. Wrist rollers are better suited for heavy wrist flexion.

Heavy Static Holds
These are one of the best ways to develop bigger forearms. Farmer's carries and static holds of 20-60 seconds allows for high loads, high tension, and high blood flow. My forearms went through their biggest transformation as a 19 year-old on a deadlift-intensive program. I gained over an inch that summer by simply deadlifting like a man for the first time.

Low-to-Moderate Grip Tension Through Range of Motion
This is where thick implements and open-hand grips come into play. The extra gripping required causes a huge pump almost instantly. I prefer to keep resistance low when taking an open-hand grip through a full range of motion at the elbow joint. High tension flowing through a moving elbow joint quickly causes discomfort and flare-ups.

Moderate to High Reps
We want to flood the forearms with blood and nutrients. Getting a good pump requires moderate to high reps: 8-20-plus reps depending on the exercise.

Be Cautious With High Grip-Tension Through Range of Motion
I've found through experience that the number one way to develop flexor/pronator mass or, if you're not careful, biceps tendinitis and pain, is by using a high-strain grip in a full range of motion exercise. This usually involves using high resistance with a pinch or open-hand grip.

I've personally suffered through four partial or full elbow ligament tears, so my elbow and forearms are a scarred mess. When you have a trashed joint, it'll let you know in a hurry when stress levels increase.

Examples are rowing with thick implements such as a fat bar or chinning on a pair of grenade balls, a rope, etc. I suspect that the cause of this excessive stress is found in the forearm flexors being forced to concurrently stabilize both the wrist and elbow joint while allowing motion in both.

Biceps curls with thick implements are also stressful, but loads are a lot lighter than rowing, so it may be more acceptable depending on the person. Have you ever tried performing a biceps curl with a heavy-resistance pinch grip? Instant pain. Fat grips are best suited for static holds and carries rather than exercises that will force the flexors to go through a range of motion under high strain.

Hit The Extensors!
The posterior compartment of the forearm contains the extensors of the wrist and hand. These need to be developed along with the flexor/pronators, but most neglect them. I recommend three key exercises to help maintain balance between forearm compartments.

Reverse Wrist Curls/Wrist Rolls

Everyone in my facility loves the wrist roller – it's task-oriented and more interactive. We mostly use reverse wrist rolls rather than wrist curls but both crush the wrist extensors. It's important to use a curl bar and semi-pronated grip on reverse wrist curls as a straight bar prevents natural motion.

Reverse Biceps Curls

Reverse curls need no real introduction. I like a mixture of medium and high-rep sets: some strength work at 4-8 reps and focus on a pump at 12-20 reps. It's important to attempt to extend the wrist while curling the weight as this makes the extensors work more actively.

Flat-Band Hand Openers

A strong crushing and pinching grip takes its toll on the finger tendons, so if maximal grip strength is the goal, these are a must. For those only looking at forearm size, reverse wrist and biceps curls will suffice.

Simple Programming
Programming is relatively simple. Mix a little bit in with your movements if you're not doing heavy pulling (a thick implement instead of plain handle, perhaps) and save the hard stuff for the end. If you train 4 days per week, your scheme might look like this:

Grip Strength
Day 1 – Heavy static holds or farmer's carries

Work up to a weight you can hold for 10 seconds; 4-6 sets are usually enough. Finish with reverse wrist curls, 4 sets of 8 reps.

Day 2 – Pinch gripping

Performing 4-6 sets of 10-20 seconds is a good starting point.

Day 3 – Gripper work

Get warmed up and build to 6-8 heavy gripping sets of 2-3 reps. Finish with band extensors for 3 sets of 20.

Day 4 – Open-hand training

Add three reps to all of your barbell assistance exercises and use a fat grip. Romanian deadlifts and rows are well suited here.

Forearm Size
Day 1 – Heavy static holds or farmer's carries.

Use a weight that you can hold or carry for 3-5 carries of 30-60 seconds.

Day 2 – Wrist curling

Hit the wrist roller or wrist curls hard, to failure, for 3-5 sets somewhere in the 15-30-rep range.

Day 3 – Reverse wrist/biceps curling

Same as day two. Hit the wrist extensors hard for 3-5 failure sets of 10-20 reps. Go a little heavier than you would with wrist flexion.

Day 4 – Open-hand training

Dedicate one pulling exercise to use with a thick implement and spend an additional 5 minutes at the end of the workout with holds or carries.

Get Those Iron Mitts
Devote 5-8 good, intense minutes to grip work before you finish your peri-workout nutrition. Do some every day using a different element above that falls in line with your goal.

If you want bigger forearms, don't waste time doing plate pinches. The load is too light, there's no pump, and it's almost all finger strength. But if you need to take down an opponent by his fight shorts, then pinch away.

Freaky Forearm Training

Every male lifter – whether he's a serious bodybuilder, powerlifter, or mid-set texting gym rat – wants muscular arms. Those who disagree are either lying or lack testicular tackle.

But while peaked biceps and horseshoe triceps get the most attention – not to mention ink in the muscle magazines – what's even more impressive, at least to me, are massive forearms.

The current programming trend among strength coaches is more compound movements and less isolation exercises. An unfortunate result of this is a lack of direct forearm training – but I'm here to tell you if you want to maximize your development and improve your performance, you need to train your forearms and your hands!

Even if you aren't an athlete, a crushing grip is vital for your performance inside and outside the weight room. Forearm and grip training will help your heavy compound lifts like deadlifts and rows, in addition to lending an extra note of intimidation to an already muscular physique.

However, forearm training isn't just about adding a few wrist curls to the end of your workout. It's important to hit all areas of the forearms and all functions of the wrist, including direct hand and finger training.

For the majority of weight room exercises, the last link between you and the bar is your hands. The stronger your grip, the more weight you'll be able to control, leading to more growth.

This is especially true with pulling movements – if your grip is a limiting factor you'll never reach your size and strength potential.

To develop total hand strength and a set of freaky forearms, it's important to hit all the categories of grip and forearm training over the course of your training cycle.

For hand training, there's support, pinch, and crush. For forearm training, there's flexion/extension, ulnar/radial deviation, and pronation/supination.

Support
Training for support grip is among the most basic ways to train your forearms. If you're not doing any direct forearm training then this likely is the only grip training that you're doing.

Jim Wendler advocates high-rep back exercises like DB rows and barbell shrugs to train the grip, while Jim "Smitty" Smith suggests performing deadlifts with a double-overhand grip as long as you can before switching to an over-under grip.

Another tip from the pros is to hold each rep at the top of a deadlift for a few extra seconds to work the grip a little more, along with performing double overhand rack pulls and Romanian deadlifts.

A favorite support training method of mine is to perform a suitcase deadlift inside a power rack by grabbing the sleeve of a heavy barbell. Go head to head with a partner and hold for as long as you can until one guy quits! Make sure to hit both sides.

Still, the king of all support grip exercises is the farmer's walk. Picking up a heavy weight and carrying it does wonders for your forearms as well as your muscular endurance, not to mention making the whole body grow.

You can perform farmers walk's with a variety of implements such as dumbbells, kettlebells, farmer's handles, or even two barbells. If you're limited for space simply pick up the weight and hold for time to work your support grip.

To work your hands even more, an open-hand challenge can be added to any of the support exercises mentioned. You can go low tech and wrap a towel several times around a barbell or dumbbell to create a thick bar, or you can add a set of Fat Gripz or Grip4orce to any barbell.

The main difference between the Fat Gripz and the Grip4orce is the Grip4orce also has a crushing element (you need to actively close them) that makes them much harder. Try adding some thick-bar training to your pulling exercises to kill two birds with one stone.

Another side benefit of thick bar training is reduced stress on the shoulders and elbows because it disperses the force over a greater surface area.

Crush

Crush grip is what most people think of as hand training. A crushing grip is extremely important for barbell lifting since it's what creates the connection between your hands and the bar. The harder you grip the barbell, the stronger your connection will be and the more stable your set up will become.

This increased stability is also going to help keep stress off the shoulders when pressing and helps you maintain better technique. The stronger your connection to the bar, the better your form will be.

One of the best ways to train for crushing grip is with hand grippers. The problem is the particular gripper you buy is either way too easy or way too hard.

One tip I got from grip training expert Jedd Johnson is to use spring loaded grippers such as the Vulcan. This allows you to adjust the grippers to suit your individual strength level just like you would a barbell.

You can make incremental jumps by adjusting the spring up or down – you can even micro progress the gripper by adding rubber bands to the top of this device.

If you're serious about developing a crushing grip, my advice is to invest in a spring-loaded gripper. This way you only need to buy one device to progressively improve your hand strength and forearm development.

One of my favorite ways to train for crushing strength is rope climbing and hand-over-hand rope pulls. Every time you grab the rope you'll have to use your crushing strength to stabilize your body and hold onto the rope.

Rope climbing and hand over hand pulls are also an awesome to supplement your current back training, with the added benefit of grip strength.

If you don't have access to a high ceiling but have a rope, you can perform recline rope climbs with a partner or in a power rack.
Big guys can get the same benefit by performing hand over hand pulls on a sled. Attach a rope to a sled and perform for time or distance.

If you don't have access to a sled, set up bands attached to a power rack and perform hand over hand pulls or supine "rope climbs."

Since not everyone has access to a rope, you can get the benefits of rope climbing by performing all forms of climbing on pull-up bars inside your power rack.

Another way to train for crushing grip is to use much thinner implements such as towels for pulling movements like pull-ups and rows. To keep a grip on the towel you need to constantly "crush" it so your hands don't slip off. This is a very low-tech solution that can really take your forearm training to the next level.

One of my favorite towel modifications is with T-bar rows as discussed in my perfect pulling exercises article. If your grip isn't quite ready for towel pull-ups, towel machine rows and inverted rows are another great options.

Wrist Postures
To have fully developed forearms, it's important to hit them from all angles and vary your direct forearm training on a regular basis.

Probably the most popular way to train forearms is with wrist curls and reverse wrist curls. The video below shows two variations of the basic wrist curl using dumbbells. Be sure to also do these from a pronated position to hit both sides of the forearm.

Perhaps my favorite way to train both wrist flexion and extension is by using a wrist roller. You can get a standard wrist roller or use bands and a barbell inside a power rack to eliminate shoulder contribution.

Make sure to perform the wrist roller in both directions to hit both sides and focus on the forearms doing the work by minimizing body English.

Anti-Flexion Extension
Whenever you perform a pressing movement with a barbell, you're constantly fighting for neutral wrist position, which also works the forearms. It's also why world-class bench pressers tend to have bowling pins for forearms.

Another way to train this pattern is any bottoms-up kettlebell exercise. When you perform cleans, presses, and snatches with the base of the kettlebell up, you must fight to resist both flexion and extension. If you have access to kettlebells, make sure you perform some bottom up work from time to time to work this pattern.

Ulnar Radial Deviations
Ulnar and radial deviation is a forgotten forearm movement, but it's critical if you want to maximize your forearm potential. You can perform ulnar and radial deviation with the wrist roller setup mentioned in the previous section.

Section 4 : Gaining Mass

Optimized Nutrition Volume, 3: building big biceps

If you're looking to add muscle mass to your frame, hitting the weights hard is a given. Quality time in the gym begins a cascade of changes that will stimulate your muscles to grow bigger in response to the challenges you throw their way. It's tempting to think that's all it takes to add muscle to your body. After all, you can actually feel your biceps growing after an intense set of curls.

That pump is tangible, real-time biofeedback to let you know that blood is flowing to your muscle cells, beginning a chain of events that stimulates protein synthesis. Maybe that's why it's easy to overlook how important good nutrition is in the **mass-building** equation. When you choose to eat, say, chicken instead of ice cream, there's no immediate muscle gratification -- no pump to keep you motivated.

Make no mistake: Eating for muscle is just as important as lifting for muscle. The foods you grab in the morning on the way to work, the meals you pack for lunch and mid-afternoon, what you put into your body immediately following your workout, and your final meal of the day impact your results as much as, if not more than, the number of reps you squeeze out at the end of a set. But in reality, it can be tough to stick to a ""clean"" diet when you're busy. We know that adding another layer of complexity to life in the form of reading food labels and studying ingredient lists just isn"t an option for most of us. Not to mention actually preparing all those healthy meals.

Optimized Nutrition Volume, 3: building big biceps

Rule #1: Calories are Key, But They're Not Everything

While it's okay to chow down on the occasional fast-food choice for convenience, a mass-gain program isn't an excuse to gorge on pizza and chocolate sundaes. ""Rebuilding muscle tissue broken down by training requires energy — in other words, calories,"" Aceto says. ""But many people, including many nutritionists, overestimate the energy needs for **gaining mass**, encouraging extreme high-calorie intakes. This often leads to an increase in body fat, making you bigger, for sure, but also leaving you fat." In general, aim for 300-500 more calories every day than your body burns through exercise and normal functioning (multiply bodyweight by 17). And that's divided among six meals a day

Rule #2: <u>Concentrate on Protein</u>

Protein is important for mass gains because it's the only nutrient that's capable of stimulating **muscle growth**. You should consume up to 2 grams of protein per pound of bodyweight daily. Eating every three hours will help ensure you're absorbing and assimilating enough protein to support muscle growth.

Rule #3: Eat After Training

"It's especially important to eat a carb- and protein-rich meal immediately after a workout," Aceto says. "Right after training, it turns out that your body is really lousy at taking carbohydrates and sending them down fat-storing pathways,"" he says. "So post-training, **carbs** will be sent down growth-promoting pathways instead."" And when these carbs are combined with a **protein source**, you've got a strong muscle-feeding combination because carbohydrates help deliver the amino acids into muscles by boosting insulin levels. This anabolic hormone drives nutrients into the muscle cells and kick-starts the muscle-growth process.

Rule #4: Stay Hydrated

Drink plenty of water throughout the day, especially in the hours leading up to your workout. This can help you feel full and reduce hunger pangs. During training, drink about 8 ounces every 15-20 minutes, more when it's hot and humid. The reason is simple: Your performance quickly begins to suffer when the body is dehydrated just 1%–2%. And if you wait till you feel thirsty, you've waited too long. A flavorful, low-calorie **sports drink** is a great way to hydrate. Try drinking fluids stored at cooler temperatures; studies show that people consume more when the liquid is colder.

Rule #5: Mass Gains Vary by Individual

Gains will differ from one individual to another depending on body size and level of experience in the gym. To make sure you're gaining muscle, not fat, don't just consider your scale weight. Instead, rely on what you see in the mirror and use a tape measure twice a month to keep track of your waist and hips (you don't want to gain there)— as well as your biceps, chest and quads. Also, don't think that you have to gain a set amount of weight each and every week. "Your mass gain doesn't have to be uniform,"" Aceto explains. That means you can gain 1/2 pound one week and 1 1/2 the next, perhaps none the third week and still remain on course. ""Expecting uniform gains ignores the intricate makeup of the body and the way it gains mass — or loses fat - which is by no means in linear fashion," adds Aceto.

Optimized Nutrition Volume, 3: building big biceps

Poundstone Power: Eat Clean, Get Jacked

A lot of people think that building the kind of strength needed to hoist a 500-pound Atlas stone or press a 242-pound dumbbell overhead means eating thousands upon thousands of extra calories—any way you can get them. It's the stigma of **powerlifting** and strongman and it's one earned over time; some of the best athletes in both sports might also make great competitive eaters.

But it's my firm belief that you don't have to pack away a bacon cheeseburger and a chocolate shake every night to be competitive in these sports. It's true that strength athletes need to consume more calories than other pro athletes, but I've learned that you can eat clean without sacrificing strength.

Look at the way bodybuilders eat: skinless **chicken breasts**, whole grains, lots of **vegetables**, all portioned out into meticulously timed meals. That clean-eating trend has reached through all levels of sport as the importance of balanced nutrition is becoming more pervasive.

The biggest problem in the diets of most strongmen and powerlifters is an intake of excess calories without balance, meaning a huge amount of animal protein paired with too few vegetables, foods that really give us the micronutrients and can help positively affect the PH of the body.

It's all a balancing act between getting the amount of protein and calories needed and trying to make it healthy by getting more bang for your caloric "buck."

We can all learn from the mistakes commonly made by strength athletes. With a little discipline and planning, it's possible to throw up some huge numbers in the gym without blowing up your waistline.

How to Eat Clean

■ Broaden Your Color Palate

Try to incorporate more foods in your diet that are colorful—this means things like peppers, leafy greens, Brussels sprouts, and broccoli. These vegetables are your body's best way to get micronutrients such as anthocyanins, carotenoids (including lycopene), chlorophyll and anthoxanthins, which are all proven to promote health.

■ Add Soy Protein

To offset the high amount of animal-based protein in my diet, I make sure my protein contains soy. Studies have shown that 25 grams of soy protein a day can help lower cholesterol. Muscles like these are made with vegetables as well as protein.

5 Things You Need to Know About Soy

Does soy really lower testosterone? Find out and learn more about this versatile food.

1) It <u>doesn't</u> reduce T Levels!

We'll get this out of the way first: **Soy** contains compounds called phytoestrogens, which are basically the vegetal version of the female sex hormone estrogen. But—and this is important—those phytoestrogens do not act like estrogen in the male body. Got that? There's ample evidence that soy doesn't reduce **testosterone levels** or ruin muscle mass.

2) It's packed with macronutrients.

One cup of edamame (boiled soybeans) contains 298 calories, 29 grams of protein, 17 grams of carbs and 15 grams of fat. One scoop of soy protein powder contains 120 calories, 25 grams of protein, 1 gram of carbs and 1.5 grams of fat.

3) It helps you recover.

Adding **soy protein powder** to both pre- and post-workout shakes is an excellent way to use soy's plentiful antioxidants to improve recovery from exercise. Add it in a 1:1 ratio with whey.

4) It increases blood flow and HGH.

It's not just good for antioxidants. Soy boosts nitricoxide levels, which increases blood flow to muscles and growth-hormone levels.

5) It makes a mean scramble.

We'd never recommend avoiding eggs, but silken tofu makes an excellent scramble. Have some leftover vegetables? Throw them in a frying pan, then beat three eggs and start them cooking before adding half a box of silken tofu to the pan. Mash it around with the eggs and veggies, add a bit of salt and you're good to go.

The Yes and No in Soy

To soy or not to soy? We debunk the myths about soy protein.

Nutrition experts used to debate the effectiveness of soy protein for promoting **muscle growth**. Critics of soy claimed that because the plant protein contains phytoestrogens—natural chemicals with a structure similar to estrogen—soy could lower **testosterone** levels and boost estrogen. But several research studies have confirmed that soy protein doesn't alter levels of testosterone or estrogen. Even a recent study claiming that soy lowered T levels was debunked.

The Benefits of Soy

Since soy protein, particularly soy protein isolate, is fairly fast-digesting and rich in arginine, the amino acid that's regularly converted to nitric oxide (NO) in the body, we now recommend adding soy to your pre-workout whey protein shake.

Research from Virginia Polytechnic Institute and State University (Blacksburg) confirms that consuming soy before training is a good idea not only because of its high arginine content but also because it directly stimulates NO production. The researchers reported in a 2008 issue of the Journal of Nutrition that genistein—one of the major phytochemicals in soy—increased the amount of nitric oxide synthase, an enzyme that catalyzes the arginine-NO conversion. Therefore, because soy protein is rich in both arginine and genistein, taking it before workouts increases NO levels and blood flow to the muscles.

Mix 10 grams of soy protein isolate with 10 grams of whey protein isolate within 30 minutes of workouts. Whey provides peptides (small proteins) that enhance blood flow by a mechanism not involving NO, so using both whey and soy will maximize blood flow to your muscles. This makes more nutrients, oxygen and anabolic hormones available to your exercising muscles and produces greater energy, a bigger pump, and enhanced recovery and growth postworkout.

Protein Prelude

Try this mix of proteins within 30 minutes before workouts for greater energy, muscle pump, recovery and growth.

Optimized Nutrition Volume, 3: building big biceps

Protein	Amount
Whey protein isolate	10 g
Soy protein isolate	10 g

7 Protein-Packed and Carb-Rich Foods

Seven foods that give you the protein and carb punch you need to gain mass.

Protein isn't the only thing you need to gain muscle mass. Don't be afraid of the carbs. But before you reach for a loaf of bread, here are seven nutrient-packed foods that give you the dose of protein and carbs that you need to get big. And they're all readily accessible at your local supermarket.

Egg Whites

Show us a bodybuilder without egg whites in his diet, and we'll show you someone who's missing out on the best protein money can buy. Paired with oatmeal, an egg-white omelet can turn your breakfast into a power meal to fuel the rest of your day.

Buy It: When purchasing eggs, do the basics: Always check the date and open the carton to check for cracks. Also, be sure the eggs are refrigerated in the store and when you get home with them. Although eggs stored out of the refrigerator won't necessarily cause illness, they do lose a grade per day when not refrigerated.

Prepare It: Although many gadgets promise an easy way to separate the yolk from the white, the quickest, easiest method is to simply use your own clean hands. For this six-egg-white omelet recipe, crack six eggs into a medium-sized bowl. Next, using clean fingers, lightly grasp the yolks, lift them out one by one, and discard. With a fork or whisk, whisk the egg whites with salt, pepper and any of your favorite herbs until well combined and a few bubbles have formed on top. Spray a medium nonstick skillet with cooking spray. Place it over medium-high heat and add egg whites. After about 15 seconds, reduce heat to medium. Pull in on the edges of the omelet with a spatula and slightly tilt the pan so the uncooked egg runs under the cooked portion. Continue this around the perimeter until most of the uncooked egg disappears. Then fold the omelet in thirds, as if you're folding a letter to fit it into a business envelope. Using the spatula, carefully slide it from the pan to a plate and eat it immediately.

Nutrients: 99 calories, 21 g protein, 2 g carbohydrate, 0 g fat, 0 g fiber.

London Broil Steak (AKA Top Round Steak)

Chicken breast may be the quintessential bodybuilding staple, but lean cuts of red meat are loaded with complete protein and pack the most punch when you're trying to pack more beef on your frame.

Buy It: Always purchase London broil that's bright-red in color. If it has even the lightest tint of brown to it, it has started to spoil. Try to find a steak or roast that's at least 1 inch thick with as little visible fat as possible.

Prepare It: Preheat a grill to the highest heat setting. Remove all visible fat and cut the steak or roast into 4-6-ounce individual steaks. Season both sides of meat with salt, pepper and/or a spice rub or marinade. Place on grill and cook 3-6 minutes per side or until cooked to your liking.

Nutrients: A 4-ounce (measured raw) lean top round steak has 138 calories, 24 g protein, 0 g carbohydrate, 4 g fat, 0 g fiber.

Salmon Fillet

Salmon has the prerequisite protein as well as the added benefits of unsaturated (good) fats. Hardcore lifters are often deficient in fats, because they're so often on super-low-fat diets. Including certain fish in your daily intake is one way to get the fats back -- at least the healthy kind.

Buy It: Atlantic salmon is the variety most commonly found in American grocery stores, and is generally the most affordable. When fresh, it's bright orange in color and doesn't feel slimy or exude an odor. Always choose a thicker cut -- because the tail gets more of a workout when the fish is in the water, the meat near the tail is tougher.

Prepare It: Be sure all bones are removed from the fillet (a "fillet" by definition is boneless, but sometimes a few stray bones don't get removed). Preheat oven to 400 degrees F. Place the 4-6-ounce fillet on a baking sheet or pan, seasoned as desired. (To practically eliminate cleanup, line the pan with aluminum foil before adding the salmon, so you can throw the foil out after it cools.) Bake 10-14 minutes or until pink in the center, and the fish flakes with a fork.

Nutrients: A 4-ounce (measured raw) serving has 207 calories, 23 g protein, 0 g carbohydrate, 12 g fat, 0 g fiber.

Chicken Breast

Why did the chicken cross the road? To get away from the hordes of bodybuilders chasing after it. Dumb joke, but it's no understatement to say that the majority of gym rats consume chicken breast on a regular basis. And why not? High in protein and ultra-low in fat, the bird's unoffending taste makes it palatable for most everyone.

Buy It: Save money by buying boneless, skinless chicken breasts in bulk in the freezer section. Be sure raw chicken is pinkish in color (not white-toned, which would indicate freezer burn or improper refrigeration). Defrost overnight in the refrigerator. The defrosted chicken shouldn't feel or smell slimy.

Prepare It: Preheat a grill to the highest heat setting. Trim all visible fat from the breast, and season or marinate it with your favorite spices or sauce. Place chicken on the hot grill (it should sizzle), then turn the heat to the lowest setting. Cook for 4-6 minutes, then flip and cook 4-6 minutes more, until no longer pink inside or a thermometer stuck into the thickest portion of the breast reads 170 degrees F.

Nutrients: A 6-ounce (weighed raw) breast has 205 calories, 38 g protein, 0 g carbohydrate, 4 g fat, 0 g fiber.

Sweet Potato

A buff body isn't built by protein alone. Carbohydrates provide energy you need to work hard and play hard. Sweet potatoes provide that oomph without overdosing your system with simple, fast-acting carbs. They're often used precontest by bodybuilders looking to fill out depleted muscles, but even if you're not getting ready for the stage, they're an excellent part of any dieting or mass-gaining strategy.

Buy It: Sweet potatoes come in two varieties: the white kind are like regular baking potatoes; the dark ones have a dark skin and orange flesh and are packed with nutrients. When choosing a sweet potato, make sure it has a smooth, firm skin with no bruises or blemishes. Stick with smaller or medium-sized sweet potatoes, which tend to taste better than jumbo ones.

Prepare It: Preheat oven to 350 degrees F. Scrub the potato under cold water using a veggie brush, making sure to remove all dirt. Pat it dry, then prick it 5-6 times all over with a fork. Place directly on a lower oven rack and bake about one hour (for an 8-12-ounce potato), or until it's soft when pierced with a fork.

Nutrients: An 8-ounce sweet potato has 240 calories, 4 g protein, 55 g carbohydrate, 1 g fat, 7 g fiber.

Pork Tenderloin

Pork is often shunned by diet purists, and what a shame. Not only is it more flavorful than chicken, but some cuts are almost as low in fat while still boasting the requisite protein power. Pork tenderloin is the filet mignon of pork -- it's the most tender, as well as the leanest portion, of the meat.

Buy It: Pork tenderloin is generally found prepacked in a plastic wrapper in the meat section of the grocery store and is usually dated. Be sure that the meat isn't expiring within a couple of days. Look for a tenderloin that feels firm, lacks a lot of visible fat and gristle, and has a tinge of pink to it. If it appears dry or even a little gray, don't purchase it.

Prepare It: Trim all visible fat using a sharp knife. Marinate the pork in your favorite marinade for one hour to overnight in the refrigerator, or coat it with your favorite spice rub. Preheat oven to 300 degrees F. Meanwhile, spray a skillet with nonstick spray and place over high heat. Brown the meat, about one minute per side, until just browned, then transfer to a baking dish and place in oven until a meat thermometer reads 155 degrees F and the meat is only slightly pink inside, approximately 15-25 minutes. Slice and serve hot.

Nutrients: A 4-ounce serving has 136 calories, 24 g protein, 0 g carbohydrate, 4 g fat, 0 g fiber.

Asparagus

Asparagus? Seriously, if you want to grow, your mom was right -- you need veggies. When it comes to greens, you have plenty of great choices. Broccoli and spinach are other highly recommended options, but we picked asparagus for its water-leaching quality. Top bodybuilders turn to asparagus as a meal when it comes down to precontest crunch time and they need to get extra-tight for the stage.

Buy It: Whether the spears are thin or thick, they should have a bright-green color and be free of blemishes and bruises. The buds at the tip should be closed tightly, not wilting. For best taste, consume within three days of purchase.

Prepare It: Trim the base of each stalk. If you've chosen thick stalks with tough skin, it's best to peel the base end with a vegetable peeler. Lay a spear flat, then, starting about halfway between the tip and base, peel to the end of the base. Rotate the spear and continue to peel the lower half until all sides are peeled and the base is about the same thickness as the tip. Select a pan wide enough to lay the spears flat, add 1 inch of water and a pinch of salt, and place over high heat until water boils. Add asparagus so that the tips all face the same end. Boil 3-4 minutes for thin spears (4-6 minutes for thicker ones), or until spears are just crisp and tender. Remove and serve hot.

Nutrients: A 4-ounce serving has 27 calories, 3 g protein, 5 g carbohydrate, less than 1 g fat, 2 g fiber.

Optimized Nutrition Volume, 3: building big biceps

8 Ways to Up Your Protein Intake
8 nutrition strategies to help you get all the protein you need for growth.

Everyone knows protein is essential to **building muscle**, but you don't always have the time to cook a meal every night or the money to constantly buy fresh meat from the butcher. If you're having trouble fitting a plan into your daily routine of working and working out, here are some nutrition-saving tips to make sure you're getting all you need to make sure your gym gains aren't going to waste with the wrong fuel.

JOIN A WAREHOUSE-STYLE STORE

The annual fee (usually 50 bucks or less) is well worth the savings you'll accrue by regularly shopping at a discount warehouse. You'll find almost all the foods on your menu at a club store, simplifying your weekly shopping trip.

BUY MEAT IN BULK

Whether you shop at a discount-style store or a regular grocery store, you can often save as much as 50 percent by buying in bulk. Whatever your favorite types of meat—boned chicken breast, lean cuts of beef or even pork—buy large discounted packages. Divide them into individual portions. Freeze most of them (make certain they're properly wrapped so they don't spoil or get freezer burn), and put those that you'll be using within a day or two in the refrigerator.

EAT FOODS THAT CONTAIN FAT

Cheese, nuts and egg yolks are great high-protein foods (and nuts and cheese, if properly stored, also stay fresh for a long time). They contain fats, making them satisfying snacks to curb junk-food or carb cravings. Reduced-fat cheese is probably the best option, but don't fear the real thing, either. Great snack choices include boiled eggs, almonds, pistachios, walnuts, cashews, mixed nuts, cottage cheese and white cheeses, such as mozzarella and Swiss.

DRINK MILK

Milk usually stays fresh for a week or two after purchase. For those times when you don't even have what it takes to mix up a protein shake, you can just pull milk out of the refrigerator. Consume 32 ounces, and you get 36 grams (g) of protein with only about 360 calories. To boost your recovery and anabolic drive, add fat-free or low-fat milk to your protein shake for an infusion of carbs.

PREP FOOD ONCE A WEEK

Doing most of your food prep once a week provides a solution to one of the most difficult bodybuilding-nutrition issues: time management. Devote a couple of hours to cooking once a week, and the rest of the week you will be able to make bodybuilding meals in a modicum of time. The goal is to prepare as much food as you can without spending all your time in the kitchen.

DEFROST IN THE REFRIGERATOR

Move meat from the freezer to the refrigerator a day before it will be cooked. It takes longer to defrost meat this way, but it will add storage life after it's been cooked (and help you avoid food poisoning). Put only as much meat in the refrigerator as you plan to cook the next day.

PREPACKAGE YOUR MEALS

Once you've cooked several portions of meat, package it so it's safe and convenient to eat. Place servings into individual containers that are safe to use in a microwave oven. (Some plastic containers are not microwavable and should be avoided.) As an alternative, place what you've cooked into one large container and parcel out your meals on a daily basis (cooked meat should safely last in a fridge for three or four days).

GRIND YOUR MEAT

Here's a GREAT way to get down two or three more chicken breasts per meal with fewer hassles: grind the meat. It makes it easier to chew, easier to swallow and ultimately easier to get sufficient protein for best case scenario growth (it speeds up absorption, helping to increase the efficiency of the protein consumed and the speed at which the amino acids arrive at the muscle cells). Cooked ground chicken makes an ideal postexercise meal (eaten about an hour after a post workout whey shake). An electric meat grinder may cost $100 or more. You can also ask a butcher to grind your meat for you. Keep in mind that once meat has been ground, it spoils more quickly, so you need to cook it soon after (the same day is the best option).

4 Lean, Protein-Packed Game Meats for Grilling

Switch up your grilling with these lean, flavorful and muscle-building game meats.

Venison

At 2.5 grams of fat per 100 gram serving, venison is a leaner alternative to beef. The key to maximizing its flavor is rich spices, says Scott Conant, owner of Scarpetta restaurant in NYC. Try rubbing the meat with cinnamon, cloves, and nutmeg, then searing over high heat.

Gator

"Treat it just like chicken," says Chris Kersch of Healthy Buffalo, a specialty meats store in Chinchester, NH. "Just make sure it's well-done. It's almost translucent when you first get it." Try rubbing a Cajun spice mix on your alligator before grilling for some real New Orleans flavor.

Ostrich

Drizzle the meat with olive oil before grilling to maintain moisture, and go easy on the spices—it's got a great natural flavor. "It's very similar to a venison flavor, although a little more mild," explains Kersch. "It's not quite as gamy and a little bit sweeter than the venison as well."

Bison

This one is going to be the easiest transition for guys hesitant to abandon the burger. "You won't really be able to tell the difference, depending on what you put on it," says Conant. "The best way I can describe the flavor is that it's similar to beef, but it's just a cleaner taste," says Kersch.

(31:5 is the average protein-to-fat ratio, in grams, of these four meats)

Quick Tips

Get a Meat Thermometer

Invest in a meat thermometer and measure internal temperature by sticking the tip of the thermometer in the center of the meat.

Optimized Nutrition Volume, 3: building big biceps

Less is More

Don't get too aggressive with the spices. Too much and you will drown out the meat's natural flavor. "Take fresh rosemary and put it in the microwave for about three to five minutes," says Conant. "When you take it out, it will literally crumble into a powder. Rub that on the meat and it will have a huge flavor."

Beat the Heat

Game meats are very lean, so if you cook them too fast the meat may dry out. Keep your grill between low and medium to ensure the best flavor.

Grill Masters 101

Take your next BBQ up a notch by grilling everything you can get your hands on.

There's a whole world out there beyond **chicken** and steak, and it's about time you started exploring, with *M&F* guiding the way, of course. From fruit and **vegetables** to a whole snapper, the list of foods you can grill is virtually endless, and as men it is our right—nay, our duty—to get as far down that list as possible.

After all, it won't be long before summer's over and it's time to retreat to the kitchen, where you've prepared your meals for the past eight months, so take advantage while you can. Gentlemen, it's time to grill everything.

Fruit

Often overlooked but always delicious, grilled fruit is incredibly easy to make. It's a fun way to promote fruit from a boring snack food to an interesting side dish, and a good opportunity to spice up typical grilled fare. Try pairing mango with chicken, or pineapple with beef or pork chops. Grilling partially dehydrates the fruit and caramelizes the sugar, which concentrates and really brings out the flavor.

Fruits like apples, pears, peaches, and figs can be cut in half and grilled facedown, or diced and skewered.

Softer fruits like bananas and mangoes can be cooked with the skin on to maintain their shape. Cook fruit over medium heat on a well-oiled grill and serve it as soon as the grill lines become pronounced.

Grill Tips:

Using your tongs, dip a rolled-up dishcloth in canola oil to prep your grill.
Cheat day? Sprinkle some brown sugar on fruit before grilling and pair with low-fat yogurt for a killer dessert.
Grill tongs are longer than kitchen tongs— usually between 13 and 22 inches

Pizza

If you've ever tried to make your own pizza, you probably did it in your kitchen oven. the grill, however, is a far better choice; the open flames mimic the conditions inside a real pizza oven, and the smoke adds complexity to your pie's flavor. In truth, it's a tough meal to mess up if you follow our recipe, which is part of what makes grilled pizza a great call when you've got people over.

Divvy up the dough and let your friends choose their own toppings and you'll be a legend in their eyes. Or grill up a couple of pies for yourself with your favorite proteins and toppings and freeze them for when fast-food cravings inevitably attack.

Ingredients:

- 6 oz chicken breast
- Pizza dough (as much as you need)
- ¼ cup wholewheat flour
- 2 tbsp olive oil
- ½ cup tomato sauce
- ½ tomato, sliced
- 1 cup toppings (mixed peppers, onion, olives, etc.)
- ½ cup low-fat cheese, grated

Directions:

1. Grill chicken breast and then cut into pieces of desired size. Set aside.
2. Stretch out dough and, on a floured surface, shape to preferred size and thickness (we recommend about half an inch).
3. Put dough, without toppings, on oiled grill, close lid, and cook two minutes or until lightly browned on the underside.
4. Remove pizza from grill and place grilled side up on nearby surface. Coat the top with olive oil. Spread sauce, then arrange all toppings, adding cheese last.
5. Put pizza back on grill and close lid. You'll know it's done when the bottom begins to char and cheese starts bubbling. Let rest a few minutes, then serve.

Grill Tips:

You can find prepared pizza dough in the frozen foods section at your local supermarket and even some pizzerias. Your grill should be hot enough that you can hold your hand an inch above it for no longer than two seconds.
55 - The percentage increase in the absorption of lycopene, a pigment found in tomatoes when they are heated, according to an Ohio State University study.

Fish

Slapping a whole fish on the grill is one of those things that would intimidate most guys. It's also something that after doing for the first time makes you realize how silly it is to be intimidated by a fish, which is about as easy to cook as any steak, sausage, or chicken breast. and in terms of survival, it's probably not a bad skill to have, either.

But since you're not in the wild, go ahead and buy a fish that has been scaled and gutted with the gills removed. We like snapper, but you can use almost any kind of fish. On your way out of the grocery store, grab a lemon, a couple of sprigs of thyme, and you're ready to grill.

Ingredients:

- 2 lb snapper
- 1½ tbsp olive oil

- Salt and pepper to taste
- 1 lemon
- 4 sprigs thyme

Directions:

1. Make three to four vertical incisions on both sides of the fish, about two inches apart.
2. Coat the fish and the inside of the body cavity with olive oil. Sprinkle salt on both sides of fish.
3. Season the cavity with salt and pepper and stuff in three or four lemon slices and thyme.
4. Throw the fish on the grill with constant medium heat and cook 10 minutes each side. Flip carefully.
5. Remove the fish from the grill, squeeze remaining lemon on top, and serve

Grill Tips:

To test doneness, insert your fork into the thickest part of the fish. it should come out warm.
Number of minutes, as a general rule of thumb, to cook each side per inch of thickness.
Oil your grill to minimize sticking. there will be some stick regardless.
This Technique works well with any of these fish: salmon, trout, grouper, walleye, bluefish, sea bream, sea bass, red drum, snapper.

Vegetables

You wouldn't exclude vegetables from a typical meal, so why leave them off the grill? Grilling brings out the best in most vegetables—some flavors intensify, others sweeten—and a few notables like corn, asparagus, onion, and peppers are rendered so delectable, they might have you empathizing with vegetarians.

Vegetables do better on the grill when brushed lightly with oil to prevent sticking, but it's not crucial if you're dealing with a well-oiled grill. Pre-grill seasoning, meanwhile, is a great way to add flavor without calories. as for the temperature, a steady medium heat is best, and resisting the urge to move your veggies around every few minutes will get you those coveted grill lines.

Grill Tips:

Cooking without foil will really amp up the smoky flavor in your vegetables.

Timing Is Everything:

Some vegetables need more time on the grill than others.

Vegetable	Grilling Time
Asparagus	5 Minutes
Zucchini	6 Minutes
Portabello Mushroom	7 Minutes
Bell Pepper	10 Minutes
White Mushroom	12 Minutes
Corn	15 Minutes

5 Best Meats to Throw on the Grill

With the grilling season upon us, check out this list of healthy, delicious, protein-packed meats that are perfect for the BBQ.

he **grilling** season is upon us, and who doesn't like a good BBQ? Your cardiologist, that's who.

That is, of course, if your cuisine consists of fatty **meats**, high in calories. We're talking ribs, pork chops, sausages, even good ole burgers and steaks. Hot dogs? Everyone's Fourth of July favorite, not to mention all processed meats are a nutritional wasteland, that the AICR (American Institute for Cancer Research) has linked to causing cancer, largely of the colorectal variety.

Not to scare you away from the grill this season, but facts are facts. Over-charring, over-smoking, even keeping an unkempt grill can affect the nutritional content of your meat. A clean grill coupled with some efficient cooking is key in serving the best quality food to your family and friends.

But which meats are the best to serve? There is a way to go clean and lean without sacrificing anything in the way of taste at the picnic table. Or rooftop floor, front porch, etc.

Here are five proteins (not counting chicken breasts, aka Captain Obvious) primed for summer grilling that will cut down on the gluttonous filling.

1) Ground Turkey Burger

A BBQ without burgers is criminal, but the same can be said for red meat in your diet. Lean to extra lean ground turkey meat is a solid substitute for beef, but it's important to remember that not all turkey burgers are created equal. Make sure to get ground turkey "breast" that is devoid of dark meat and skin, if you really want to cut the fat. And to avoid the dreaded dry turkey burger, mix in some olive oil to the patties (3 to 5 ounces in size), cook them quickly at roughly 165 degrees, and finish them off with a slice of white American cheese.

Nutritional Info (per 5 oz):
Protein - 41g
Fat - 3.5g

Carbs - 0g
Calories - 196

2) Pork Tenderlion

Everyone loves a good pork chop. Too bad your average cut is lined with a fortress of fat that seeps through the entire slab. A 4-ounce pork chop contains 275 calories and 16 grams of fat. By comparison, a 4-ounce serving of pork tenderloin (a lean strip located on the backbone) contains 120 calories and just 4 grams of fat. It's a drastic difference, not to mention the tenderloin is loaded with protein (22 grams per serving) resulting in some serious fat burning. Before laying it out on the grill, give the tenderloin a nice dry rub consisting of some oregano, garlic powder, ground cumin and dried thyme.

Nutritional Info (per 5 oz):
Protein - 22g
Fat - 4.6g
Carbs - 0g
Calories - 137

3) Flank Steak

For some people, standard BBQ fare of burgers and hot dogs just doesn't cut the mustard. When it comes to grilling snobs, steak will always reign supreme. With respect to the red flag on red meat, if you want to incorporate some steak into your BBQ at least go with a lean cut. Flank steak is a great (and cheap) example – low in fat and calories compared to other steaks, while also being rich in protein (23 grams per serving) and iron. While not ideally tender, a lean meat like flank steak can be softened up with a marinade consisting of Worchester, soy, or chili sauce. Here's a great idea: grill the meat and slice it diagonally for some steak tacos, topped with some grilled onions and peppers and fresh guacamole.

Nutritional Info (per 5 oz):
Protein - 39g
Fat - 10g
Carbs - 0g
Calories – 260

4) Swordfish

Of course, if you want to go super-healthy (i.e., low in fat/calories) at your BBQ, fish is always the best way to go. But which fish is best fit for the grill? Our answer is swordfish; a beautiful steak that is meaty and firm and perfect for the rigors of backyard broiling. Swordfish is versatile, in that it can simply be prepared with some olive oil, lemon, salt and pepper, or can be marinated in a variety of different (healthy) sauce options. Best of all, swordfish's dense texture makes for perfect grill marks. Just make sure not to cook it any longer than 5-7 minutes, to prevent the meat from drying out.

Nutritional Info (per 5 oz):
Protein - 33g
Fat - 11g
Carbs - 0g
Calories - 244

5) Pheasant

For a more exotic form of fowl at your BBQ, ditch the grilled chicken for some wild or farm raised pheasant. The lean game bird's caloric content is made up of 78 percent protein, and the meat is also high in B vitamins and potassium. To maximize the healthiness, shed the skin and grill the tiny bird as you would a whole rotisserie chicken. While pheasant is low in the white meat department, it is still a lean option for your BBQ that packs a smoky taste very conducive to the grilling process.

Nutritional Info (per 5 oz):
Protein - 45g
Fat - 17g
Carbs - 0g
Calories - 335

Build Muscle With Fall Foods

Fall food doesn't mean it's loaded with carbs and fat. Try these healthy and hearty seasonal foods.

It's the same story every year; summer ends, and the months give way to colder weather, less daylight, holidays, heartier food, and other excuses to **cheat** when it comes to diet and **exercise**.

Avoiding the Fall Lull

But is the fall season really our enemy? While seasonal affective disorder is in fact a thing—in which the autumn and winter months bring on a "seasonal depression" that saps energy and increases consumption—it is combatible with a proper diet. While it's easy to associate fall foods with high fat and calorie counts, the harvest brings a plethora of fruits and vegetables rich in fiber and vitamins.

Seamus Mullen is the chef/owner of Tertulia in NYC, and author of *Hero Food*, a health cookbook released last year. Mullen is well aware of the "comfort food" tendencies that accompany fall, simply from observing his customers. "We definitely gravitate towards longer evening meals in the fall," says Mullen. "We see it in the restaurant all the time—people come in earlier for dinner and have longer meals. There is something 'hearty' about eating a large meal when it's cold and dark outside."

While we all love having a nice hearty meal on a cold night, Mullen encourages eating most of your calories during the day while making an effort to have lighter, more digestible meals in the evening. This is so our bodies can rest and recover while we sleep, rather than work hard to break down a huge meal.

"It takes a lot effort to remind ourselves to curtail unhealthy habits like overeating at night, but once a good habit is set in place, it becomes so much easier to maintain," says Mullen. "Breaking the habit is the hardest part."

Embrace Fall Food

According to Mullen, the best way to steer clear of bad habits is to embrace stews and braises, as well as all the wonderful fall vegetables that come into season. "The one thing to be aware of is that many of the root vegetables, like beets, parsnips, and rutabaga, while delicious and full of nutrients, are also rather high on the glycemic index," says Mullen, "so its good to balance them out with some cruciferous greens and vegetables from the brassica family, like Brussels sprouts."

For choice meat cuts, fall is a great time for lamb and pork, according to Mullen, which if naturally raised, are great sources of good fats and proteins.

And how does a little bacon sound in your fall diet? "Lately, I've been really into making warm bacon vinaigrettes," says Mullen. "Good bacon is good for you in moderation, and a bacon vinaigrette is a great way to maximize the bacon flavor, without eating a pound of the stuff."

Just dice up some bacon, render it in a pan, and add a little mustard, honey, and cider vinegar, while whisking in a little olive oil, and you've got a "terrific warm vinaigrette to drizzle over a salad of shaved apples and shaved cabbage," says Mullen. "Healthy, tasty, seasonal."

Here are some fall meal recipes rich in seasonal ingredients and flavor, compliments of Chef Mullen.

Grilled Lamb Loin with Shaved Brussels Sprouts Salad and Chia Seed Cider Vinaigrette

Spice-crusted Grass-fed Hanger Steak with Olive Oil Sweet Potato Mash & Radicchio Pomegranate Slaw

Soft Scramble of Pastured Eggs with Grass-fed Butter, Avocado, Chia Seeds, Smoked Wild Salmon and Tuscan Kale

Grilled lamb loin with shaved Brussels sprouts salad and chia seed cider vinaigrette.

Servings:

4

Ingredients:

2

lamb loins, about 8-10 oz each preferably naturally raised and grass fed

1/2 cup

olive oil

2

cloves garlic, crushed to a paste

1

branch rosemary, leave finely minced

1/2 tsp

red pepper flakes

salt

and fresh pepper

For the salad

1 pound

Brussels Sprouts, shaved paper thin on a mandoline or with a food processor

Optimized Nutrition Volume, 3: building big biceps

1

Apple, I like Braeburn or Winesap apples, finely sliced

1

shallot, finely sliced

4

radishes, thinly sliced

2 tbsp

fresh mint, minced

2 tbsp

fresh basil, minced

salt

and pepper to taste

For the vinaigrette

1/3 cup

cider vinegar

2 tbsp

raw honey

1 tsp

Dijon mustard

1 clove

garlic, minced

1 tsp

chia seeds

2/3 cup

Extra virgin olive oil

Instructions:

1. Combine all ingredients except olive oil and whisk in the olive oil until fully incorporated. For the salad combine all ingredients, season with salt and pepper and drizzle with the vinaigrette. Grill the lamb on both sides until nicely marked and medium rare in the center. An instant read thermometer should show about 140 F in the center. Remove the lamb and let it rest on a cutting board for a few minutes, then slice. I like to toss the lamb in with the salad and add all the resting juices for extra flavor. Serve right away.

2. Pre-heat grill to medium high.

3. Season the lamb loins on all sides with kosher salt and fresh ground pepper. Combine olive oil with rosemary, garlic and pepper flakes and thoroughly cover the lamb loins with the mixture. Set aside to marinate for a few minutes as the grill heats up and you prepare the salad.

4. For the salad combine all ingredients, season with salt and pepper and drizzle with the vinaigrette

5. Grill the lamb on both sides until nicely marked and medium rare in the center. An instant read thermometer should show about 140 F in the center. Remove the lamb and let it rest on a cutting board for a few minutes, then slice. I like to toss the lamb in with the salad and add all the resting juices for extra flavor. Serve right away.

Spice-Crusted Hanger Steak

Spice-crusted grass-fed hanger steak with olive oil sweet potato mash and radicchio pomegranate slaw.

Servings:

4

Ingredients:

4

grass fed hanger steaks, about 6-8 oz each

1 tbsp

ground coriander seed

1 tbsp

ground mustard seed

1 tbsp

ground fennel seed

1 tbsp

whole sesame seed

4 tbsp

olive oil

Kosher salt and fresh ground pepper

4

sweet potatoes, peeled and simmered in salted water until tender

1

clove garlic, crushed into a paste

4 tbsp

extra virgin olive oil

salt and pepper to taste

1

head radicchio, thinly sliced

1

pomegranate

1 tbsp

fresh basil

2 tbsp

champagne vinegar

4 tbsp

extra virgin olive oil

salt and pepper to taste

Instructions:

1. For the steaks, season each steak with salt and pepper. Combine all the spices and sesame seeds and coat each steak thoroughly. Pre-heat the olive oil in a cast iron pad over high heat until it begins to smoke then pan roast the steaks for about two minutes on each side, no more than 5 minutes total. Remove to a cutting board and allow to rest for a few minutes.

2. For the sweet potatoes, with a fork or a potato masher, combine all ingredients and season with salt and pepper to taste.

3. For the slaw, toss the radicchio with the pomegranate seeds and season with salt and pepper then add the basil and drizzle with the vinegar and olive oil to taste.

4. Slice the steak with a sharp knife against the grain and serve over the sweet potato mash and finish with a small garnish of the slaw. Serve immediately.

Soft Scrambled Eggs

Soft scrambled eggs with grass-fed butter, avocado, chia seeds, smoked wild salmon and Tuscan kale.

Servings:

2

Ingredients:

5

Pastured eggs, lightly beaten

2 tbsp

unsalted grass fed butter, cut into small pieces

1 tsp

chia seeds

Optimized Nutrition Volume, 3: building big biceps

1 tbsp

fresh dill leaves

4

leaves Tuscan kale, thinly sliced

1

clove garlic, thinly sliced

1 tbsp

olive oil

2 oz

Smoked Wild Salmon, thinly sliced

1

avocado, cut into 1/2 " pieces

salt and pepper to taste

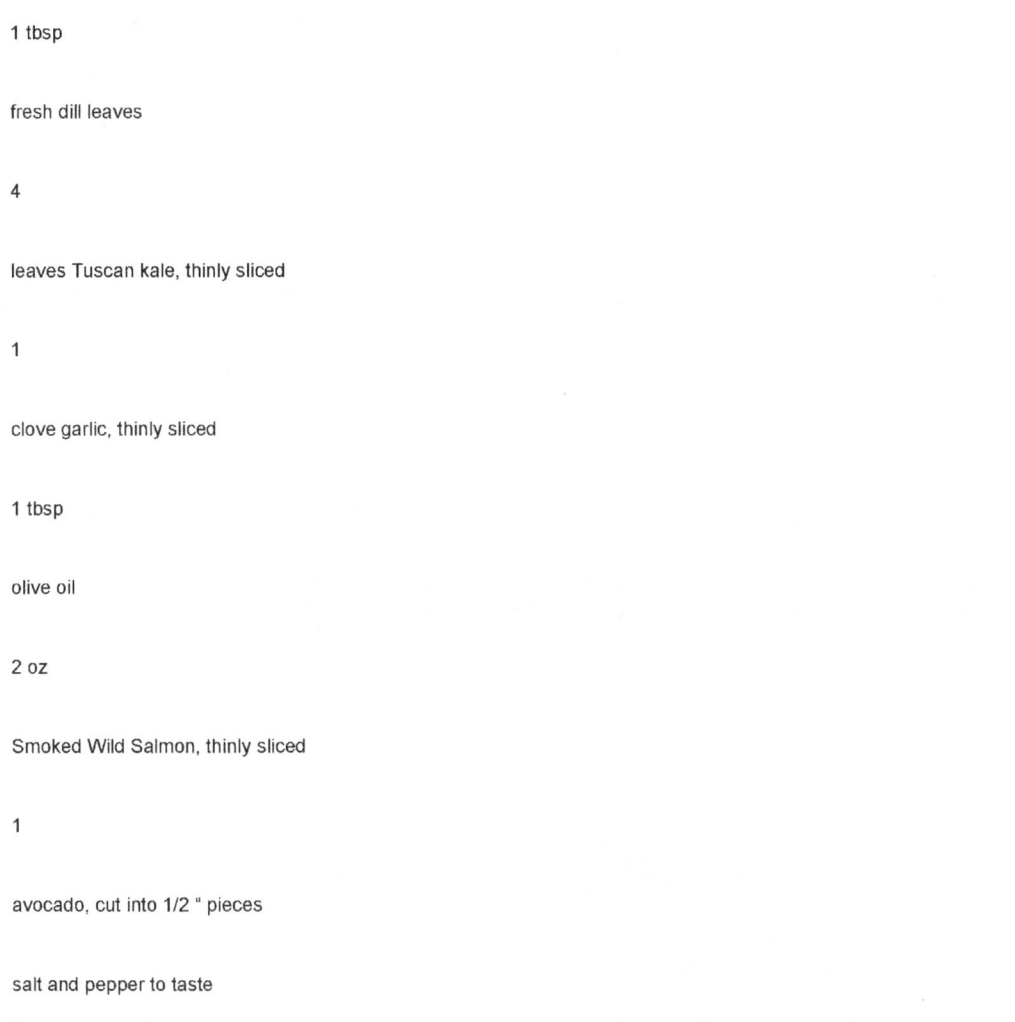

Instructions:

1. In a medium sized mixing bowl, combine lightly beaten eggs with butter, dill, chia seeds and Smoked Salmon.
2. Heat the olive oil over medium low heat in a medium sized non-stick or well seasoned cast iron pan.
3. Add the kale and gently wilt, about 1 minute. Add the garlic and sweat for another minute then add the egg mixture.

4. With a heat-resistant rubber spatula, gently fold the eggs together until creamy and lightly scrambled, but still a little moist.

5. Fold in the avocado at the very last minute and serve right away

5 by 5 Meal Plan: Gain 5 Pounds of Muscle by Cinco de Mayo

Keep your eye on the prize and you can pack some muscle onto your frame in 4 weeks. Let us help you.

Set a clear goal, and stick to it. Make it a theme. Let's gain 5 pounds of muscle by 5/5. In all, we have about 4 weeks, so it's crunch time. I don't care how you see it, but I'm not only looking at the weight on the scale, anybody can gain 5 pounds on the scale. However, we need 5 pounds of **lean muscle mass** and metabolically active tissue in 4 weeks.

Test Your Body Fat Percentage

First off, get your **body fat** done by a professional, not with the cheap bio-impedance scale you have in your bathroom. Here's a quick look at how to measure body fat:

Skinfold calipers: Cheap and easy. However, get a seasoned trainer, since accuracy builds with the number of tests done on different individuals. Takes about 5 minutes to complete.
Dexascan: Expensive, accurate but not easy to find near you. Since you have to repeat the test in 4 weeks to see how you have done, maybe not the way to go.
Hydrostatic weighing: Not practical but very accurate. It's rare you can find someone or a special lab who does it, and it takes about 20 minutes.
Anthropometric: Easy, cheap but inaccurate. You can't really tell if you have lost fat or gained lean mass.

For your purposes, skinfold calipers are the way to go. There are many methods, but any of them, if done properly, always at the beginning of the week and at the same time of day, can accurately track your progress.

Optimized Nutrition Volume, 3: building big biceps

Training Split

Now that we know where we're starting, let's see how to reach our goal. First, your training protocol. It goes without saying that the main goal is hypertrophy. Keep your rep range between 8 to 1 and use your workouts to create as much damage as possible. You need to train 4 to 5 days a week, one or two body parts per day, incorporating drop sets, the mechanical advantage principle, supersets and short rest periods to maximize muscle growth.

Week 1 - 4 sets of 8-10 reps
Week 2 - 3 sets of 10-12 reps and add 1 or 2 more exercises per body part
Week 3 - 5-6 sets of 6-8 reps. Use 3 major exercises per body part. Arnold said it best, as soon as he added more volume to his routine, growth was the outcome.
Week 4 - Make it a hell week. Supergiant sets. Choose 5 exercises, do 10 reps of each, in a circuit style training one after the other, repeat for 5 sets.

For those with time on their hands and a bit of insanity in their brains, try two-a-days. Training time for each session should be no more than 30-40 minutes. Morning sessions are limited to one or two exercises and afternoon sessions can have 3 to 4 exercises.

AM training: low reps, high volume
PM training: high reps and supersets, low volume

Example:
AM workout Chest = 8 total sets of 3-5 reps with 120 seconds rest between sets
PM workout Chest = 6-7 total sets of 8-15 reps with minimal rests between sets

Determining Your Nutritional Needs

With both training protocols, your results should come fast enough, however, the most important aspect of your 4 weeks is the nutrition protocol. Let's make some simple rules for the plan:

1. Eat at least 1.5 to 2x your weight in pounds of protein. The protein turnover will make sure you gain lean muscle mass as well as regenerate, and repair other important tissue.
2. Our post workout shakes will be Uber important
3. Veggies at every meal of the day
4. Simple carbs at night for diner is allowed. (example to follow)
5. 4 workouts a week 4-5 feedings a day
6. 5 workouts a week 5-6 feedings a day
7. At least 3 liters of water a day

8. Under any circumstance, do not skip meals

9. Fat is not the enemy

10. Rule number one is the most important

If you weigh 200 pounds, your daily caloric needs should go beyond 2500 calories a day; if you train twice a day, 3000 calories should be the goal. You should eat at least 300 to 400g of protein a day. Keep complex carbohydrates throughout the day such as green veggies with some medium to higher glycemic index foods such as potatoes, yams, and wild rice in the afternoon and lunch. I am a big fan of the Charles Poliquin meat and nuts breakfast. It sets up your neurotransmitters on high efficiency and stabilizes your sugar throughout the day. Better insulin control means improved muscle and ATP re-synthesis and more energy for your next workout.

Tips

- If you train in the morning, eat your breakfast as usual, an hour or two later hit the gym, then save the shake for post-workout.

- If you train at night, make your post-workout shake your last meal.

- You don't need to have tons of carbs to gain mass. Focus on quality instead of quantity.

- Don't be scared of fats. Your joints will thank you for it. Keeps your testosterone at optimal levels, which you obviously need to gain lean muscle tissue.

- Suggested pre-workout supplements: BCAA, Beta-Alanine

- Suggested post-workout supplements: BCAA, Fenugreek, Magnesium, Vitamin C

- Keep in mind that this is no one size fits all plan. You might want to play with macronutrient ratios. Add carbs, remove fat, increase protein, add a meal. Take notes of everything and next time you'll get even better results.

The Meal Plan

Here is the nutrition plan with macro nutrient breakdown:

Meal 1

- 6 oz ground beef

- 1 handful of almonds
- 1 med apple

Calories: 597
Proteins: 59g
Carbohydrates: 29g
Fats: 30g

Meal 2

- Protein shake with at least 60g whey isolate
- 1 cup of berries
- 1 tbsp of coconut oil

Calories: 500
Protein: 60g
Carbohydrates: 20g
Fat: 15g

Meal 3

- 6oz turkey breast
- 1 cup cauliflower
- 1 cup green beans
- 1 large tomato
- ½ avocado
- 1 tbsp olive oil

Calories: 610
Protein: 65g
Carbohydrates: 38g
Fats: 28g

Meal 4

- 4oz salmon
- 1 cup cooked brown rice

- 1 cup Kale
- 1 cup asparagus
- 1 tbsp olive oil

Calories: 624
Protein: 50g
Carbohydrates: 58g
Fats: 25gr

Meal 5

- Protein shake with at least 60g whey isolate
- 1 cup of berries (or other fruit)
- I handful of walnuts

Calories: 500
Protein: 60g
Carbohydrates: 20g
Fat: 15g

Total Calories: 2810
Total Protein: 300g
Total Carbohydrates: 166g
Total Fats: 115g

I don't believe in trying to keep the same ratio of macronutrients throughout the day since different bodies require different needs. What I had the most success with is tweaking macros for individual needs. You might find that you can deal best with carbs in the morning but others might want to commit sleep suicide when they eat too many carbohydrates for breakfast. I go for function and energy. It always was and always will be a trial and error game. If you do it right, you'll keep that fresh new muscle mass for a while, and you'll lose fat in the process.

Optimized Nutrition Volume, 3: building big biceps

Protein Face-Off

Four proteins enter, one protein leaves. Today, settles the age-old debate on which protein is the clear-cut, gram-for-gram champion.

Many people consider whey to be the hands-down, gram-for-gram winner in the world of **protein powders**. Quick digestion, high branched-chain amino acid content, great effects on protein synthesis - it's hard to debate the billing. But unlike boxing managers who duck some fighters for fear of an upset, we're not afraid of a little competition. As such, we're tossing all four of the top proteins into the ring for a no-holds-barred, fact-by-fact fight for the ages.

You, the huddled masses yearning to be ripped, crave an authoritative protein champ. Like fight fans, you probably have your loyalties. Some of the old troops who long for the days of Ali and Frazier might still be clinging to egg white protein for their fix. Others might be fond of the new-school science that favors **casein**, whose steady Oscar de la Hoya-like reliability has been enough to fortify their physiques. And then there are those of you who are starting to root for the underdog. Despite its less-than-impressive ring record, **soy** - like a surging contender - is a protein on the rise and has scored some impressive victories of late. But like the great Marciano, whey's dominance in this division of sports nutrition has been unrivaled - ...until now.

This fight will be decided in 10 rounds, or categories, each with a separate but distinct focus that goes to the heart of protein effectiveness. Unlike boxing's 10-point must system, however, we're going for golf scoring - low score wins. The winner of each round is awarded one point, second place gets two, third gets three and, if you're still following, fourth gets four. We'll tally the points from each category, and the protein with the fewest points will be Protein Powder Champion. If all the challengers are ready, it's time to touch gloves and fight it out. You want to ring the bell?

Round 1: Amino Acid Content

A complete protein is composed of 20 different amino acids, and some of those are more critical than others. At the top of that list are the branched-chain amino acids (BCAAs) that include leucine, isoleucine and valine, which are musts for protein synthesis, the process by which muscle fibers grow. Arginine is crucial for stimulating production of nitric oxide (NO), which has numerous vital properties for muscle growth, such as increasing blood flow to muscles to deliver more nutrients, anabolic hormones and oxygen for better recovery and greater muscle protein synthesis. Glutamine is also high on the list because, along with a multitude of other benefits, it keeps muscle protein synthesis high and muscle protein breakdown low. In a hard-fought opening round for amino acid content supremacy, check out the tally:

SCORECARD

>> **No. 1** Whey: Due to its higher content of BCAAs - particularly leucine, the most critical amino for stimulating protein synthesis - whey is the clear winner in this opening round.

>> **No. 2** Soy: The highest of the four in arginine content, and second to whey and casein in leucine and glutamine contents, respectively, soy comes in second.

>> **No. 3** Casein: The highest in glutamine, casein comes in third. It'll have to put up a stronger fight moving forward if it expects to stay in the hunt.

>> **No. 4** Egg White: Although egg white has a great overall amino acid mix, it's highest in none of the most critical amino acids but is second to soy in arginine.

Round 2: Bioavailability

The true test of a protein is bioavailability - how much of its critical aminos actually make it to the muscles. To measure this, scientists use the protein digestibility corrected amino acid score (PDCAAS). It takes into consideration the amino acid content of the protein and its digestibility, which ensures the aminos get to muscles. Proteins that meet the amino acid and digestibility requirements for humans get a PDCAAS of 100%. All four proteins featured here meet the requirements for humans. In other words, they're high-quality protein sources unlike, say, black beans, which get an 84%. Here's how the battle of bioavailability shakes out:

SCORECARD

>> No. 1 (Tie) Whey, Casein, Soy and Egg White: The PDCAAS of each protein is 100%.

Round 3: Health Benefits

For bodybuilders, the No. 1 reason to use protein powders is to boost muscle growth. But you may be surprised to find that some of the proteins have multiple health benefits. Time for the underdog to flash its health assets:

SCORECARD

>> No. 1 Soy: Soy reigns in the top spot here in the third. Not only does it protect against cardiovascular disease, but the FDA-approved health claim for 25 grams of soy protein daily reduces the risk. Soy is also beneficial in protecting against numerous cancers such as colorectal, breast and prostate.

>> No. 2 Whey: Although the extra health benefits of soy may not get some bodybuilders to use it more often, many guys will be happy to know that the whey protein they love for mass-gaining also does a body good. For starters, because it comes from milk, it's a good source of calcium, which enhances bone and dental health as well as aids fat loss. Whey was also recently found to reduce the risk of cardiovascular disease via its ability to lower blood pressure and increase blood vessel dilation, which has muscle-building effects. In addition, whey enhances the body's levels of a critical antioxidant known as glutathione and may even help ward off certain cancers. Whey protein also lowers LDL (bad cholesterol) levels.

>> No. 3 Casein: Similar to whey, casein contains beneficial peptides that help lower blood pressure; it's also a good source of calcium. Not bad, but not enough to climb ahead on the scorecards.

>> No. 4 Egg White: There's little research on the specific health benefits of egg white protein, putting it in last here.

Round 4: Pushing Protein Synthesis

Protein builds muscle by increasing the process of protein synthesis. Therefore, bodybuilders should be taking protein powders that maximize protein synthesis. During a protein synthesis-heavy fourth round, here's how the challengers stack up:

SCORECARD

>> No. 1 Whey: The landmark 1997 French study from the Universite Clermont Auvergne reported that due to whey's rapid digestion, it leads to significantly higher protein synthesis than casein. Although the other proteins weren't directly compared, it can be assumed that since they aren't as rapidly digested as whey, they don't stimulate protein synthesis as significantly.

>> No. 2 Soy: There's some controversy over soy's effectiveness in stimulating protein synthesis and therefore muscle growth, but in this round soy played to its strengths. Research on both bodybuilders and rats has shown soy is about as effective as whey at stimulating muscle growth. Yet research also shows that due to the slightly lower BCAA content of soy compared to whey, soy doesn't activate critical factors involved in protein synthesis as well as whey does.

>> No. 3 Casein: Although casein was shown to be less effective at stimulating protein synthesis at rest in the 1997 French study, more recent research from the University of Texas Medical Branch (Galveston) reports that casein may be just as effective at stimulating protein synthesis postworkout as whey.

>> No. 4 Egg White: Research shows that egg white protein has similar effects on stimulating protein synthesis as milk protein in certain populations. Although it has a decent amount of BCAA content, its ability to drive protein synthesis isn't as effective as that of whey.

Round 5: Stopping Muscle Breakdown

A protein's ability to stifle muscle protein breakdown is very important. That's because muscle growth is the result of the delicate balance between protein synthesis and protein breakdown. The more synthesis and less breakdown you have, the more muscle growth you'll experience. Here's how the four proteins stack up for limiting muscle protein breakdown:

SCORECARD

>> **No. 1** Casein: The French study mentioned in Round 4 also discovered that casein was superior at blunting muscle protein breakdown. This is due to its slow and steady rate of digestion, which means it delivers a continuous supply of aminos to muscle cells. Because of this, casein comes in at No. 1 here.

>> **No. 2** Egg White: The digestion rate of egg white protein isn't quite as slow as casein's, but it's also not nearly as fast as those of whey or soy. This likely leads to egg white's ability to effectively prevent muscle protein breakdown almost as well as casein as shown in clinical trials.

>> **No. 3** Soy: Soy protein digests almost as rapidly as whey, which means its ability to halt muscle protein breakdown is limited.

>> **No. 4** Whey: As effective as it is at boosting protein synthesis, whey has little effect on halting muscle protein breakdown, bringing it in at No. 4.

Round 6: Preworkout Perfection

Research shows that the most critical times to take protein powders are immediately before and after workouts. The question many bodybuilders have is, which one at which time? Here's how they compare as preworkout supplements:

SCORECARD

>> No. 1 Whey: Whey protein contains components that enhance dilation of blood vessels, which promotes the delivery of nutrients (such as the amino acids it supplies), hormones and oxygen to muscles during exercise. Due to its rapid digestion rate and impact on blood flow, its aminos are quickly available to enhance muscle protein synthesis. Research from the University of Texas Medical Branch (Galveston) shows that rapid delivery of amino acids to muscles immediately before workouts maximizes muscle protein synthesis. This brings whey in at No. 1.

>> No. 2 Soy: Soy is beginning to show signs of improvement here in the sixth. Because it has a high amount of arginine (almost 2 grams per 20 grams of soy), it makes a great preworkout protein for boosting NO levels and enhancing dilation of blood vessels. Plus it's digested almost as rapidly as whey protein.

>> No. 3 Egg White: Egg protein is second to soy in arginine content, meaning that it can also help enhance blood flow to muscles via greater dilation.

>> No. 4 Casein: Last, but certainly not least, casein is slowly digested, which means it won't get a boatload of aminos to your muscles fast. It will, however, supply a steady flow that can help stave off muscle breakdown during a workout. It comes in at No. 4 here, but it's still a valuable protein for a preworkout mix.

Round 7: Postworkout Power

It's vital to get in protein immediately postworkout to stimulate protein synthesis at this critical time. Here's how the challengers stack up as postworkout supplements:

SCORECARD

>> No. 1 Whey: Whey boosts insulin higher than the other three proteins. Because insulin is an anabolic hormone that kicks up protein synthesis, it's ideal to boost it right after a workout. Whey also has the highest levels of leucine, which is critical for muscle growth.

>> No. 2 Casein: Although researchers originally thought casein should be the last protein powder to take postworkout due to its slow digestion, more recent science showed it can stimulate protein synthesis as well as whey when taken after exercise. And one study found that adding casein to whey results in significantly more muscle than taking whey alone.

>> No. 3 Soy: Research shows that soy protein also leads to a fairly significant boost in insulin levels, just not quite as high as with whey. Soy protein's high antioxidant component helps protect muscles from oxidative damage, which can lead to less muscle damage and enhanced recovery. Not a bad round for soy.

>> No. 4 Egg White: Although egg is a quality protein, it doesn't significantly boost insulin levels. In addition, not as much research exists on its postworkout benefits.

Round 8: Muscle Building While You Sleep

You essentially undergo a 7-8-hour fast when you sleep. But taking the right protein powder before bed can make all the difference in muscle mass. Which one makes bedtime its business?

SCORECARD

>> No. 1 Casein: Casein sends the other three proteins to the mat in this round. Because it's the slowest-digesting protein powder you can buy, casein is the best choice to take right before bed. This helps supply your body with a slow drip of amino acids that can be used as fuel throughout the night, meaning your body won't turn to muscle aminos for fuel. And any amino acids from the casein not needed for fuel can boost muscle growth.

>> No. 2 Egg White: Although the digestion rate of egg white protein isn't nearly as slow as casein, it's also not as fast as whey's or soy's. Since this round is about how slowly a protein digests, egg white comes in at No. 2.

>> No. 3 Soy: Due to its rapid rate of digestion, soy makes a poor bedtime protein source. Still, it's in better shape than whey protein.

>> No. 4 Whey: Though whey has dominated the scorecards up to this point, it lost steam here in the eighth. As the fastest-digesting protein powder out there, it's the worst possible nighttime protein.

Round 9: Palatability

For some guys, benefits of certain protein powders are moot if they don't taste good and go down easy. This round compares the availability of flavors of each protein as well as their ability to mix easily in water. In the taste round, whey begins to pull away:

SCORECARD

>> **No. 1** Whey: Whey is highly soluble, meaning it dissolves well in liquids. It not only mixes well but also works with numerous flavors, such as the standard chocolate and vanilla plus fruity flavors such as watermelon. Whey protein comes in the widest range of flavors, making it No. 1 in palatability.

>> **No. 2** Soy: Close to whey in solubility, soy protein mixes fairly well in fluids. This allows availability in a variety of flavors, especially with the more recent boom in the popularity of soy.

>> **No. 3** Egg White: Egg protein is much less popular today than it was before whey's domination, which means you can usually find it only in the standard chocolate, vanilla and maybe strawberry. Still, it mixes fairly well in water.

>> **No. 4** Casein: The reason casein is a slow-digesting protein is because it forms clumps in the stomach. When you add it to a glass of water it does the same thing, making it hard to mix in water and sometimes difficult to consume. Manufacturers are making more flavors due to casein's sudden popularity surge, but it's still limited in the available flavor category.

Round 10: Price is Right

Last and certainly not least for most guys when it comes to protein selection is price. Everyone would like to fork out $50 to listen to Jim Lampley call the blow-by-blow action on HBO pay-per-view, but sometimes you have to settle for the basic cable clashes on ESPN's Friday Night Fights. Budgets for protein powders are similar - of course you want the best, but ultimately it has to be affordable. Here's how our contenders stack up on price:

SCORECARD

>> No. 1 Whey: The economics of whey protein is simple supply and demand. Demand for whey increased so much that supply eventually overshot it, leaving a ton of whey available and causing prices to drop dramatically. Today you can get a straightforward whey protein fairly inexpensively, with most 2-3-pound tubs coming in between $25 and $40. Let's see the other proteins slip that punch.

>> No. 2 Soy: Before the benefits of soy were recognized, it was simply considered a cheap protein. With more demand for soy today and better manufacturing processes that allow the production of higher-quality soy isolates, soy prices have come up. Yet it's still a fairly inexpensive protein.

>> No. 3 Casein: Once a fairly cheap protein, casein is a bit more expensive today. That's due to the more widely known value of slow-digesting proteins and the ability of manufacturers to create extremely slow-digesting caseins such as micellar casein. This brings casein in at No. 3 in the price round.

>> No. 4 Egg White: Egg white protein always has been - and still is - a high-quality but expensive protein.

The scorecards are in. For the particulars of the decision, let's go back to our official ring announcer Michael Buffer: "Ladies and gentlemen - ...a round of applause for all four of these fantastic protein options. After 10 rounds of heated and informative scientific debate, we go to the scorecards. Meeting or exceeding the criteria for a quality protein in nearly every conceivable category and coming in with the lowest tally tonight is the newly crowned, undisputed protein champion of the world - whey protein!"

Thanks, Mike. Now here's your peek at the scorecards. Remember, the low score wins.

No. 1 Whey (17 points)
No. 2 Soy (21 points)
No. 3 Casein (25 points)
No. 4 Egg White (31 points)

Post-Fight Analysis

Although whey protein was the solid winner in our bout, it doesn't mean you should buy whey as your only protein. Each of the four proteins has specific benefits unique to it.

For those on a budget who can afford just one type of protein, your best bet is a whey protein powder. But if you can afford it, consider buying a jug of whey, a jug of soy and a jug of casein, and use about 10-15 grams of each whenever you take your protein. Or check out a protein that already provides a mix of these three. Either way allows you to take advantage of each protein's high points.

As you can see, egg white - the defiant Evander Holyfield of protein that simply won't go quietly into that good night - may have been at its best years ago but is still a beneficial protein. Most bodybuilders likely get enough egg white protein from breakfast, but if you don't, consider also buying an egg white protein and adding it to your protein mix, or getting a mixed protein with egg white protein in it.

So in summary, don't ignore soy, casein and egg white. Just make sure you have whey fighting for you every day in your physique pursuits.

The $100 Diet
Lose fat, gain muscle, and get your diet in line - All for just a C-note a week.

Rent. Car payments. Car insurance. Credit cards and cable television. Living expenses add up, and by the end of the week, there's not much left to cover the one thing humans need the most: food. Question is, how do you afford to eat a high volume of meals without sacrificing the crucial nutritional principles that support all the training you do?

For most guys, tight budgets make shopping at popular organic food stores impossible, but eating fast food will sap your energy and make you fat. No matter your budget or how many time constraints you're living under, highly processed foods will never produce the results you want. Get ready, then, to eat better than you ever have, even if you're on the strictest budget. Welcome to the $100 Diet.

Macros on a Micro Paycheck

To categorize and classify foods, it's important to know which macronutrients— proteins, fats, or carbs—are in what foods. Once you're clear on that, you can build a strategy for shopping and daily meal selection.

Proteins

With the $100 Diet, you'll be spending most of your grocery money on meat. The most cost-effective protein sources for our purposes are chicken, eggs, and beef. Add fish to your shopping list as your budget allows. Whey protein is another great way to get high-quality, antioxidant-rich protein into your body quickly. It's not budgeted into our $100 Diet, but it's a good idea to use it whenever you can.

Fats

There are four types of dietary fats: trans fats, which are found in processed desserts; saturated fats from animal-based foods; monounsaturated fats found in cooking oils; and polyunsaturated fats, which must be supplemented into the $100 Diet because the body can't produce them itself.

Carbs

When your training regimen demands energy for intense, long-duration exercise, eating carbs is vital. Your carb sources for the $100 Diet will be sweet potatoes, bananas, raw oats, black beans, and fruit.

reens & Vegetables

These high-fiber foods suppress hunger and stabilize your blood sugar, and they're a vital source of micronutrients. Because these foods are easy to digest, increasing the amounts you eat will allow you to avoid the "food comas" caused by carb-based diets.

How to Budget, How to Shop

First off, you'll need to find time to cook—and by cooking, we're talking about bulk food prep on Sunday night. Cook all your meats and slice enough vegetables for three days, to ensure quick prep times for your daily meals.

The list we're providing here will trace a path around the perimeter of your grocery store, getting you in and out in 20 minutes or less and avoiding the middle aisles—which will drain both your checkbook and your health.

Your $100 Diet Grocery List

Animal Protein

4 lbs hormone-free chicken	$21.96
5 lbs ground beef	$12.45
4 dozen hormone-free cage-free eggs	$7.96
TOTAL	$42.47

Fats

2 small jars natural peanut butter	$6.58
2 large avocados	$1.79
1 bag omega trail mix	$4.69
1 bottle olive oil (8.5 oz)	$2.55
TOTAL	$15.61

Fibrous Carbs & Nutrient-Rich Foods

2 heads organic broccoli	$2.49
3 large bell peppers	$2.69
2 bags French green beans	$1.99
1 large bag organic spinach	$1.99
TOTAL	$9.16

Optimized Nutrition Volume, 3: **building big biceps**

Carbohydrates

1 bag sweet potato fries	$2.29
5-lb bag sweet potatoes	$2.69
2 cans black beans	$1.99
6 large bananas	$1.14
6 large apples	$3.54
2 lbs raw oats	$3.99
TOTAL	$15.64

Cooking Spices & Misc. Items

Cayenne pepper	$3.25
Cracked pepper	$2.25
Green tea bags	$3.12
Hot salsa	$2.99
Coffee	$3.74
Limes	$2.00
TOTAL	$17.35
FINAL TOTAL	**$100.13**

Timing it Right

The real artistry of any diet plan involves understanding your body's hormonal situation, then aligning it with proper food choices. The first step here is knowing which macronutrients you need at specific times. After compiling your comprehensive shopping list, knowing what foods you'll need when and which foods you'll need to avoid will essentially take care of itself.

Morning Meals

Upon waking your body is hormonally set up to burn fat better than it is at any other time of day, so any movement that occurs will be fueled primarily by fat. Your testosterone and growth hormone levels surge at about 9 a.m. each morning, and you don't want insulin to derail the positive impact these hormones have on your body. As a result, your breakfast should consist of protein sources, vegetables, and fats. There's really only one rule to follow in the morning: Don't eat carbs.

Afternoon Meals

Your $100 Diet midday meals will depend on whether you train in the morning or the evening. For morning training, eat the bulk of your daily carbohydrates at this meal. If you're training later in the evening, consume a large serving of vegetables and fibrous carbohydrates at midday—and always include a protein source. Then, toward the end of your workday, but at least 90 minutes before training, have some blended oats or fruit with a protein shake.

Evening Meals

Once you've finished working and training, it's time to eat in a way that will give you the energy you'll need for the next day's intense training session. Dinner is when you'll want to eat a large carb serving that's aligned with your body-composition goals. To lose weight, go for more fibrous carbs— fruit, oats, beans, or sweet potatoes— and finish your meal with lots of protein and vegetables. After-dinner snacks should contain only protein and fat to keep you in an anabolic state as you sleep.

Optimized Nutrition Volume, 3: building big biceps

Now What?

You've bought everything on your list, and now you're standing in the kitchen, broke, with eight bags of groceries and no clue what to do. Don't worry: The menu items in our meal plans are strategically selected to provide your body with precisely what it needs at the right times during the day. Follow the appropriate plan to the letter, and watch your energy levels, body composition, and strength skyrocket like never before.

Morning Training Sessions

Drink 20 oz of water each meal, more during training

Meal 1
- Shake: 8 oz coffee, 8 oz water, 2 tbsp peanut butter, and 2 scoops whey (preferably chocolate)

Training Session
- 1 apple if needed

Meal 2
- Omelet: 6 egg whites or 6 whole eggs, 1 cup spinach, 1–2 tsp hot salsa, ½ mashed avocado

Meal 3
- 8–10 oz chicken breast or ground beef (Marinate all meat in olive oil, cayenne pepper, limes, and pepper.)
- 1 cup green beans or 1 cup broccoli
- 1 cup black beans or 2 bananas

Meal 4
- ½ cup trail mix
- Hot green tea

Meal 5
(if following morning is a training session)
- 1 large sweet potato or 1 cup black beans
- 10–12 oz chicken breast or ground beef
- 1 bell pepper or 1 large spinach salad

Meal 5
(if following morning is off)
- 10–12 oz chicken breast or ground beef
- 1 cup broccoli
- 1 cup green beans

Meal 6
- 2 scoops whey
- 2 tbsp peanut butter

Evening Training Sessions

Drink 20 oz of water each meal, more during training

Meal 1
- Omelet: 6 egg whites or 6 whole eggs, 1 cup spinach, 1–2 tsp hot salsa, ½ mashed avocado

Meal 2
- 1 apple
- Shake: 8 oz coffee, 8 oz water, 2 tbsp peanut butter, and 2 scoops whey (preferably chocolate)

Meal 3
- 8–10 oz chicken breast or ground beef (Marinate all meat in olive oil, cayenne pepper, limes, and pepper.)
- 1 cup green beans
- 1 cup broccoli
- Hot green tea (Drink as your meal ends or sip throughout afternoon.)

Meal 4
- 1 cup blended oats
- 2 scoops whey
- 8 oz coffee

Training Session
- 2 bananas (Begin eating in small bites 15 minutes into your workout.)

Meal 5
- 1 large sweet potato or 1 cup black beans
- 10–12 oz chicken breast or ground beef
- 1 bell pepper or 1 large spinach salad

Meal 6
- Shake: 2 scoops whey, 2 tbsp peanut butter, 10–12 oz water

Rest Day Meal Plan

Drink 20 oz of water each meal, more during training

Meal 1
(if program goal is fat loss)
- Shake: 8 oz coffee, 8 oz water, 2 tbsp peanut butter, and 2 scoops whey (preferably chocolate)

Meal 1
(if program goal is mass gain)
- Omelet: 4–6 egg whites or whole eggs, 1 cup spinach, 1 tsp cayenne pepper, 1 tsp olive oil
- 3 oz chicken breast

Meal 2
- Hot green tea (Sip throughout afternoon.)

Meal 3
- 8–10 oz meat
- Large spinach salad
- ½ cup trail mix

Meal 4
- 8 oz chicken
- ½ avocado
- Hot green tea (Drink as meal ends or sip throughout afternoon hours.)

Meal 5
- 1 cup black beans
- 10–12 oz ground beef
- 1 cup broccoli or 1 cup green beans

Meal 6
- Shake: 2 scoops whey, 2 tbsp peanut butter, 10–12 oz water

Optimized Nutrition Volume, 3: building big biceps

Diet 911: Lean Muscle Mass Meal Plan

Crushing weights isn't the only factor in gaining lean muscle. This nutrition plan will have you packing on the muscle mass in no time.

Everyone knows crushing weights won't get you anywhere if you don't have the right diet to match. Even if you think you're eating all the right things, taking all the right supplements and getting all the right nutrients at the right time, there might be some adjustments you can make to reach your goals faster. That's where we come in.

This week, Eric Falstrault, founder of **BODHI Fit** in Montreal, Canada, takes a look at a meal plan from *Muscle & Fitness* reader Jonathan Rein. Think you've got a bulletproof diet? Submit it to **Diet911@muscleandfitness.com** and one of our nutrition experts will take a look.

*"Thought I'd share this. It needs some tweaking since I'm going for muscle gains. In terms of supplementation, I do use 1/2 scoop of **Muscle Pharm Assault**, 150 mg **Fish Oil** and a **Multi-Vitamin** pre-workout and **Glutamine** both before AND after. Any tips/fixes would be great!"*

Hey Jonathan, when it comes to gaining lean muscle mass, many factors need to be taken into consideration such as stress, digestion, supplementation, sleep and training. Never forget that in the gym we tear up fiber and damage the muscle, so our goal is to repair and regenerate as fast as possible. Getting the right nutrients into your cells is tricky and needs will never be the same for two individuals and will change from time to time.

Breakfast/Pre-Workout:
4:00 AM

Protein Shake with:

- 1 scoop **ON 100% Whey**
- 1 cup skim milk
- 1 teaspoon flaxseed
- 1 banana

Post-Workout:

6:45-7:00 AM

- 4 egg whites & 1 egg

- Cup of spinach
- 1/2 cup of oatmeal with 1 teaspoon of flaxseed and 1/4 cup of blueberries

The skim milk in your shake might sound like a great idea, but all the micro filtration and pasteurization of skimmed milk causes hidden digestive problems such as bloating or blood sugar problems. A study compared fat free milk with whole milk in post-workout shakes by measuring concentrations of representative amino acids in response to milk ingestion. This study found that whole milk was a better choice because the uptake of amino acids threonine and phenylalanine were greater for those who drank whole milk, thus increasing the efficiency of the available amino acids for protein synthesis. So if you can't take out milk from your daily regimen, whole milk would be a better alternative.

I would save the shake for post-workout. After a great training session, getting nutrients into the cells fast is key for less DOMS (delayed onset muscle soreness) and faster recuperation. A solid meal takes a bit longer to digest, thus not getting into the muscle fast enough. Switch your two first meals and get better results. Your pre-workout meal will ensure you to have steady blood sugar levels during your workout and your post workout shake will provide all the nutrients needed for tissue repair.

Mid-Morning Snack:

9:00-9:15 AM

- 1 cup Greek yogurt
- 1 large apple

Lunch:

Noon

- 6 oz. baked salmon with field greens
- 1/3 cup of homemade trail mix (soy nuts, almonds, raisins, unsweetened cherries)
- 2 carrots
- 1 pear

Mid-Afternoon Snack:

2:30 PM

- Protein Bar (Syntha-6)
- 1 large apple

As the saying goes, an apple a day keeps the doctor away, but I believe that moderation is key. Even though fruits are good for you, some are a major source of fructose. Small amounts of fructose can be easily metabolized by the liver, but a higher intake will result in fat storage, which is not the kind of mass you want to gain. Research has shown that diets with higher amounts of glucose often result in visceral fat, meaning fat around the organs, which slows down the metabolism—not good for fat loss and muscle gains. Limit yourself to one piece of fruit for your post-workout meal. Choose fruits that are low on the glycemic index such as berries or red grapes. The rule of thumb for the best body composition is to limit fructose to 10-20 grams a day. One apple has about 10 grams of fructose.

However, when you take out something of your diet, you have to add something back. Since you don't have too much vegetables in your diet, this would be the perfect time to add them. But don't just eat salads—go for the nutrient-dense vegetables such as broccoli, cauliflower, or anything that has dark green leaves. You might also consider adding color to your salads with green, yellow or red peppers.

Dinner:

5:00 PM

- 6 oz. grilled chicken breast
- 1 medium sweet potato
- 1 cup of salad with raspberry vinaigrette

Before Bed:

7:30 PM

Protein Shake, consisting of:

- 1 scoop ON 100% Casein
- 2.2/3 cups of ice
- 1 cup skim milk
- 1 teaspoon flaxseed
- 1 banana
- 1 teaspoon fresh peanut butter

FINAL NOTES:

Your diet is balanced and well timed out. If you have a steady flow of energy during the day, you are on the right track. If you have times during the day where you feel sluggish or lack focus, you might have to look back at what you ate hours before.

Your protein and fat intake seem fine, but the best way to know if you gained lean muscle mass is to have a skilled trainer take regular body fat measurements. If you know your body fat percentage, you also know how much lean muscle mass you have. You can also track if what you have been doing for the past few weeks have given you results, then you can tweak accordingly. Good luck Jonathan on your quest and keep up the great work!

Diet 911: The Drinking Man's Dilemma

You like a brew but you know alcohol slows muscle growth. What can you do? Read on to find out.

There's no way around the fact that alcohol slows muscle growth. That said, there are options for minimizing the effects of your social life.

First, supplement with **N-acetyl cysteine (NAC)**. One of the stresses that alcohol places on your liver is antioxidant depletion. Metabolizing alcohol uses up glutathione, an amino acid that serves as one of the body's strongest free-radical fighters. Taking 500–600 milligrams of NAC daily can help replenish antioxidants while clearing out toxic metabolites that are generated by the liver's breakdown of alcohol.

Another supplement to try is **leucine**. Alcohol blocks muscle building at the genetic level by inhibiting the action of leucine, the most anabolic of the branched-chain amino acids. Taking a dose the day after drinking can help override this inhibition.

Finally, try to time your drinking. Research from Penn State shows that alcohol decreases protein synthesis by 15% to 20% after 24 hours, but not sooner.

It may sound crazy, but having a few drinks on Friday night after training is better than having them on Saturday night (when your body is recovering).

The Drinking Man's Diet

Eat like this on days you indulge

Breakfast

- 3 whole omega-3 eggs and 3 egg whites, scrambled
- 1 cup FiberOne cereal
- 1 cup 2% plain Greek yogurt
- 2 tbsp slivered almonds

Meal- Replacement Shake

- 2 scoops vanilla protein powder
- 1 banana
- 5 strawberries
- ¼ cup chopped walnuts
- 2–3 cups water
- 3–4 ice cubes

Lunch

- 6 oz grilled skirt steak, fat trimmed off
- 1 cup black beans
- 3 tbsp salsa - 1 diced tomato, 2 chopped scallions, 1 tbsp extra-virgin olive oil

Post-Workout Shake

- 60–70g dextrose/maltodextrin blend
- 5g creatine
- 30g whey protein
- 15g BCAAs

Dinner

- 8 oz roasted chicken breast
- 1 baked sweet potato with 1 tbsp butter
- ⅓ cup brown rice (dry measure)
- 8 –10 asparagus stalks

Before Bed

- 20–32 oz water
- 500–600mg NAC
- 5–8g leucine

TOTALS:

Carbs - 309g
Fat - 101g
Protein - 240g
Calories - 2,951

Beer Can Strengthen Muscles

Beer can keep your muscles stronger, longer, but you'd have to pay the ultimate price.

Good news for all beer-lovers out there—beer can actually make your muscles stronger! Well, that is, if you're up for the challenge of drinking 154 pints a day.

A recent study conducted by Japanese scientists at the University of Tokushima showed that the flavonoid ingredient found in beer known as 8-prenylnarigenin (8-PN) significantly limited muscle atrophy in debilitated laboratory mice. The mice that were given the flavonoid saw minimal muscle loss compared to other mice that weren't. The control group experienced a 10 percent decrease in muscle mass.

But don't run to the store and pick up a six-pack just yet. In order to see the effects of this study on a human body, you'd have to drink so much beer—154 pints, to be exact—that you'd die of alcohol poisoning first.

In a more practical sense, scientists are now looking for alternative ways to get the daily dose of 8-PN necessary for the muscle-building benefits without the alcohol poisoning side effects. This could mean a huge breakthrough for elderly people suffering from severe muscle loss, preventing astronauts' muscles from atrophying while in space and even for paralysis patients.

While beer isn't the ideal fitness beverage of choice because of its high caloric content, it does offer other health benefits. Dark beer in particular contains more antioxidants, vitamins and minerals that have been proven to keep heart disease at bay.

Optimized Nutrition Volume, 3: building big biceps

8 Unexpected Muscle-Building Foods

These surprising food choices can help you build muscle and stay fit.

We all know that what you eat can either make or break your fitness goals. By providing your body with the raw nutrients it needs, you can ensure that your muscles are getting fed correctly in order to grow. Every bodybuilder knows the usual "**bodybuilding foods**" like the back of their hand—**chicken breast**, salmon, **eggs**... and the list goes on. However, there is an array of unconventional food options that fit-minded individuals can benefit from. Here is a list of 8 unexpected exercise foods that can help you **build muscle** and stay fit.

Quinoa

Pronounced keen-wah, this food has the highest amount of protein than any other grain. With a nutty flavor and chewy texture, quinoa makes the perfect health-conscious substitute for rice.

Try a bowl of quinoa as the perfect accompaniment to this broiled salmon and spiced yogurt recipe >>

Broiled Salmon With Spiced Yogurt Sauce

Get a healthy dose of Omega-3 oils and Vitamin D from this muscle-building fish dish.

Calories:

345

Protein:

31g

Fat:

20g

Carbs:

10g

Servings:

2

Ingredients:

2 6-oz.

salmon fillets with skin (preferably wild)

Optimized Nutrition Volume, 3: building big biceps

1/4 tsp.

coarse salt and black pepper

Nonstick cooking spray

1/3 cup

low-fat plain yogurt

1/2 Tbsp.

olive oil

1 tsp.

finely grated lime zest

1/2 Tbsp.

lime juice

1/2 tsp.

finely grated orange zest

1/2 Tbsp.

orange juice

1/2 tsp.

curry powder

1/4 tsp.

cayenne pepper

1/2 Tbsp.

honey

Equipment:

- Aluminum foil

Instructions:

1. Preheat broiler. Line rack of broiler pan with foil and lightly coat with cooking spray.

2. Rinse and pat fish dry. Sprinkle fish with salt and pepper, then broil 4 inches from heat for 7 minutes.

3. While salmon broils, whisk together yogurt, olive oil, lime and orange zest, lime and orange juice, curry powder, cayenne pepper, and honey in a bowl until combined.

4. Cover salmon loosely with foil and continue broiling 7-9 minutes or until fish is light pink throughout and flakes easily. Serve topped with yogurt sauce.

Oysters

This creature of the sea is loaded with iron, a hemoglobin-building mineral, which is needed to disperse oxygen throughout the body. A lack of iron can cause a dramatic decrease in energy levels, making it a task to drag yourself to the gym. Even worse, the lack of oxygen can cause working muscles to excrete lactic acid, making you tire more quickly.

Optimized Nutrition Volume, 3: **building big biceps**

Try this grilled oysters with spinach and feta recipe >>

Nutrition Info Per 6 medim raw oysters CALORIES ▶ 74 FAT ▶ 1G PROTEIN ▶ 5G CARBS ▶ 2G

Boost testerone and get an edge in the gym with one of the world's most polarizing foods.

Oysters are a love-it or leave-it food— some people can't get enough, and others can't stand the thought. One thing that isn't up for debate, however, is the nutritional benefit these **shellfish** pack for hard-training guys.

They're low in calories (12 per oyster) and saturated fat (less than a gram), and pack a gram of protein each. This is a boon for **bodybuilders trying to get lean**— the fat-to-protein ratio beats most whole-food proteins out there, says Jim White, R.D.

Oysters are also high in zinc, at about 6mg per. "Zinc serves as a vital mineral in the production of testosterone, and is beneficial to the proper development and maintenance of the male hormone," White says. "More testosterone means stronger lifts and more muscle." Other essentials in oysters are vitamins A through D, B12, phosphorus, calcium, and iron.

White suggests a dozen raw oysters as an appetizer, and using them as a great substitute for bread and butter. "With a dozen raw oysters, you're getting in more protein, fewer carbs and less fat, and a lot of vital nutrients," White says.

Calories:

308

Protein:

23g

Fat:

18g

Optimized Nutrition Volume, 3: **building big biceps**

Carbs:

23g

Servings:

2

Ingredients:

1 dozen

oysters

1

small shallot, chopped

2

cloves garlic, crushed

1 tbsp

olive oil

2 lbs

spinach leaves

1 tbsp

toasted pine nuts, chopped

1/4 cup

crumbled feta

Instructions:

1. Preheat grill to medium. Shuck oysters and save bottom shells.

2. Sauté the shallots and garlic in olive oil until translucent. Add the spinach and sauté until tender. Add nuts and set aside.

3. Place oysters in reserved shells. Spoon spinach mixture over the oysters, then sprinkle cheese over spinach mixture.

4. Grill on the half shell for 5–10 minutes. Serve immediately.

Apples (With Skin)

A recent study found that a natural compound found in apple skins known as ursolic acid increased muscle mass in healthy mice. The study also found that the compound reduced obesity, cholesterol, and blood sugar. Apples as a whole are an excellent source of fiber. The soluble fiber found in the "meat" of the apple reduces cholesterol and the insoluble fiber found in the skin speeds the passage of food through your stomach.

Raisins

In need of an energy boost? Pick up a box of raisins to get a healthy dose of carbs and potassium, one of the most underrated minerals for fitness buffs. Potassium helps prevent muscle cramping and dehydration, a serious concern for someone pushing their limit. It helps naturally maintain fluid balance so you can work harder in the gym.

Chia Seeds

These tiny members of the mint family have recently become the talk of the town because of their newly discovered array of health benefits. They are the richest plant source of omega-3s, containing a unique type called stearidonic acid, which converts into EPA to aid muscle recovery and inflammation. Chia seeds are also made up of 20% protein and are thought to aid in weight loss.

Ginger

Skip the medicine cabinet and opt for this natural remedy when your muscles are aching from an intense workout. This potent anti-inflammatory root can decrease swelling and prevent joint stiffness. It has also been shown to aid with weight loss, as it enables you to feel fuller, longer.

Try this ginger-chile chicken stir-fry recipe >>

Ginger-Chile Chicken Stir Fry

If you're rushed for time, this Asian-inspired recipe is just for you.

The secret behind a successful stir-fry is to prepare all of the ingredients in advance and cook them quickly. Cook the rice, chop the veggies, add the chicken, and in minutes you'll have a homemade meal. Enjoy!

Calories:

234

Protein:

27g

Fat:

7g

Carbs:

22g

Servings:

4

Ingredients:

2 tbsp

oil (divided)

1 lb

boneless, skinless chicken breasts, cut into ½-inch pieces

2 tbsp

fresh minced ginger

1

fresh Serrano chile, seeded and sliced into strips

1

medium onion, halved lengthwise and sliced into strips

1

small red bell pepper, seeded and julienned

1

small green bell pepper, seeded and julienned

1

small yellow bell pepper, seeded and julienned

¼ cup

reduced-sodium soy sauce

2 tbsp

water

2

cloves garlic, minced

2 tsp

cornstarch

1 tsp

sugar

Equipment:
- Wok or large skillet

Instructions:

1. Heat 1 Tbsp. oil in a wok or large skillet placed over medium-high heat. Add chicken and stir fry until almost cooked through. Remove chicken to a plate; cover to keep warm.

2. Heat remaining oil in wok. Add ginger, chile, onion and bell peppers; stir-fry five minutes or until peppers are crisp-tender. Return chicken to wok.

3. Mix soy sauce, water, corn starch, and sugar together in a small bowl. Pour sauce into wok and cook until sauce is thick and bubbly, about two minutes. Serve over rice.

Cherries

This bite-sized fruit is packed with exercise-friendly nutrients. The polyphenols in cherries help decrease damage to your cells caused by free radicals during intense exercise. They also contain an array of B-vitamins, which help convert nutrients into energy. Other benefits include combating post-workout soreness, easing the pain and inflammation of swollen joints, and helping you stay asleep longer.

Kefir

Pronounced kee-fer, this fermented milk beverage is similar to yogurt in that it is derived from cultures of bacteria and yeast. However, unlike yogurt, kefir has 3 times the amount of probiotics, which help boost your immune system. It's also packed with protein from whey and casein, both of which are needed to build muscle tissue.

5 Things You Should Know About Avocados

Think you know everything about this super food? Think again!

1) A whole, medium-size avocado (about five ounces) has 226 calories and contains about three grams of protein and nine grams of fiber.

2) More than 80% of an avocado's calories comes from fat, most of which are healthy, monounsaturated fats. One of those fats—oleic acid—has been shown to reduce cholesterol levels.

3) While the banana is most famous for potassium content, a typical avocado contains 35% more potassium (684 milligrams vs. 505) than that of its long, yellow cousin. Avocados are also a decent source of calcium and magnesium, crucial electrolytes for athletes because of their role in muscle function and fluid balance.

4) Every avocado contains nearly 20 vitamins, minerals, and phytonutrients—nutrients derived from plant material that provide a defense against cancers, heart disease, and signs of premature aging.

5) Regular consumption of healthy fats like the ones found in avocados has been shown to promote a boost in testosterone and growth hormone production.

Brazilian Nuts - The One-Stop Shop for Selenium

Why getting mega amounts of a minor mineral could make a big difference in your physique.

They say big things come in small packages, and the same is true for selenium. Known as a trace mineral because it's needed in only scant amounts, selenium is found primarily in plants, particularly from soil that's rich in the element, and in some meats and nuts. While it may seem minor to be deficient in a trace mineral, it can have major consequences.

Selenium is a powerful antioxidant that combats the damage that free radicals cause in the body, and it can improve cardiovascular health and fight cancer as well. It also plays a role in thyroid health, assisting with the metabolism of iodine and the production of critical thyroid hormones.

Since the thyroid controls the body's metabolism, keeping it in good working order is essential to maintaining a lean physique. But selenium can also impact that lean physique by increasing muscle strength. In a study published in The American Journal of Clinical Nutrition, researchers measured hip flexion, leg extension and grip strength in 891 subjects, and found that those who had high selenium levels were more likely to be stronger than those with lower selenium levels.

While taking supplemental selenium is the best way to ensure you get adequate amounts, it's not entirely necessary to add another pill to your supplement regimen. Brazil nuts are known to include as much as 95 mcg of selenium per nut. Given that the RDA for selenium is 55 mcg and we recommend getting 200 mcg daily, just a couple of Brazil nuts could have you set.

Since megadoses of selenium can negatively impact your health, take no more than 400 mcg per day, the upper limit set by the National Academy of Sciences Institute of Medicine (Washington, D.C.). In another nod to Brazil nuts, New Zealand researchers found that eating them was just as effective at raising selenium levels as taking a supplement. The scientists gave subjects either 100 mcg of selenium from a supp, 100 mcg of selenium through Brazil nuts or a placebo. After 12 weeks, the subjects taking the supplement or eating the nuts had blood levels of the mineral that were 60% higher. Both groups also showed increased blood levels of glutathione peroxidase, a critical antioxidant enzyme that depends on selenium to function properly.

Brazil nuts aren't the only source of selenium, just one of the best. Wherever you get your selenium, make sure you're getting enough.

Seeking Selenium? The best sources of the mighty mineral:

Optimized Nutrition Volume, 3: **building big biceps**

Food Amount Selenium, Content (mcg)

- Brazil nuts, dried, unblanched 1 oz. (about 6) 544
- Tuna, light, canned in oil 3 oz. 63
- Beef, cooked 3.5 oz. 35
- Cod, cooked 3.5 oz. 32
- Turkey, light meat, roasted 3.5 oz. 32
- Beef, chuck roast, roasted 3.5 oz. 23
- Chicken breast, roasted 3.5 oz. 20
- Macaroni, boiled 1/2 cup 15
- Egg 1 medium 14
- Low-fat (2%) cottage cheese 1/2 cup 12
- Instant oatmeal, cooked 1 cup 12
- Brown rice, cooked 1/2 cup 10
- Whole-wheat bread 1 slice 10
- Cheddar cheese 1 oz. 4

Bodybuilding Protein Alternatives

There's more to feeding your muscles than just chicken and beef. How about... deer?

Any of us who've put an ounce of thought into the process of growing and maintaining our muscles have also downed more than our fair share of poultry, beef, eggs and tuna and for many, the routine has gotten a tad bit tiresome by now. Sure, the majority of you eat to live (or better put, "**eat to get jacked**"), but variety *is* the spice of life, and who doesn't enjoy a little extra flavoring now and then?

Fortunately there are a number of **protein sources** available to us today, and many of them are of as high a quality in terms of their muscle-building properties as the old standbys. Consider spicing up your diet with these protein alternatives from time to time...

Soy

During the 1960's and 70's soy protein was a popular, inexpensive supplement popular with budget-minded bodybuilders looking to expand their range of protein sources. By the 1980's, however, it fell out of favor with those who feared its estrogen-like compounds, called isoflavones. Concerned that soy might force them into women's competitions, male bodybuilders shunned this vegetable protein.

A study presented at the 2005 Experimental Biology conference in San Diego, California, revealed that not only did test subjects on soy protein grow as much muscle as their whey-consuming brethren, they showed no decrease in serum testosterone levels. Boys will be boys, even on soy.

Fortunately for you, soy is as plentiful as more traditional bodybuilding staples tuna and chicken, particularly at natural food grocers like Trader Joe's and Whole Foods. Next time you're in L.A. you can satisfy your Jones for soy at Real Food Daily, which serves a tasty tofu wrap, along with a host of other grain protein dishes.

Bison

Although this impressive ungulate was hunted to the brink of extinction 115 years ago it's since made an impressive comeback, both on the American Great Plains and Americans' plates. Packing a protein to fat ratio similar to tuna and skinless chicken breast, buffalo is tastes a bit like beef, but it is a little drier, due to its lower fat content.

Bison meat, unlike some of the other protein sources to follow, is fairly easy to get, be it in the Trader Joe's frozen foods section, Whole Foods or at your local butcher's shop. Or, the next time you're in Manhattan, New York, you could stop by one of the six Heartland Brewery locations for a hearty, free-range, grass-fed bison burger to go with a microbrewed pale ale.

Crustaceans

Most of us think of crustaceans either as sea bugs or things to be savored on first dates and business dinners. Fact is though that lobster, shrimp and crab can provide a great protein-rich boost to your humdrum diet.

For example, a 100-gram serving (about 3-1/2 ounces) of shrimp will yield you 21 grams of protein and just a single gram of fat, with no calories to count for your ketogenic diet. Crab and lobster are similarly stocked with that most potent of muscle-building nutrients.

If cost is a consideration (for whom isn't it?) we suggest you check the freezer of your local supermarket where you can find 3 lb. bags of frozen shrimp at a price comparable to chicken breast. And the next time you find yourself with a hankering for crustacean be sure to get yourself to the nearest Chart House (there are 27 across the country), where you can savor mouth-watering lump crabmeat, shrimp cocktails and lobster tail. Who said protein had to bore the palate?

Ostrich

Ostrich meat has a taste unto itself and, like bison, is exceptionally high in bodybuilder-friendly protein. Although the ostrich is clearly a bird (albeit a very, very large one), its taste more closely resembles that of beef than chicken. Ostrich steaks turn a rich reddish hue when cooked and they often have a speckled appearance from the insertion points of their large feathers.

Ostrich isn't as readily available as bison, yet most quality butchers should carry filets and/or ground meat. You could also stop by Catelli Ristorante and Cafe in Voorhees, New Jersey, which serves ostrich both as an appetizer and an entrée. Because of its red meat taste, we suggest that you try it with a nice shiraz. *Buon appetito*!

Venison

Venison, a.k.a. deer meat (elk is also referred to as venison), has a long history of sustaining man, most notably woodland-dwelling Native Americans, for whom it was a staple. Leaner than beef and generally more tender, venison can be used to make sausages, jerky, roasts and filets.

While venison is widely available throughout European supermarkets, it's less readily available in the United States — although specialty butchers and sites like venisonsteaks.com and elkusa.com can meet your deer meat needs. For the hardcore venison aficionado, a trip to Banff, Alberta's The Grizzly House might be in order. There you can not only order a seven ounce venison steak, but get your fix of frog, shark and boar, too — all excellently exotic sources of protein in their own right.

Approximate Nutritional Comparisons of Various Protein Sources

100 Grams (Lean, Cooked)	Protein*	Fat*	Calories*	Iron† (Mg)	Cholesterol† (Mg)
Ostrich	32.2	1.2	111	4.9	65
Bison	28.5	2.5	143	3.42	82
Venison	29	2	144	3.7	66
Chicken (skinless)	28.9	7.4	190	2.1	89
Turkey (skinless)	29.3	5.0	170	1.8	76
Beef (select)	29.5	8	201	2.99	86
Pork	29.3	9.7	212	1.1	86
Sockeye salmon	27	11	216	.55	52
Tuna	30	6	184	1.26	49

12 Rules of Big Eating

Follow these guidelines to ensure your muscle-building hard work in the gym doesn't go to waste.

Here's some simple math that many people still can't seem to grasp. You're in the gym for only an hour or so each day, leaving another 22–23 hours in which muscle growth depends solely on what goes in—or stays out of—your piehole. So why is the **nutrition** side of the **mass-gaining** equation often marginalized? It's probably because a bench press is a lot sexier than a spinach salad. But if you want to take your physique from string bean to Mr. Clean, certain dietary principles need your utmost attention. These 12 get-big eating tips will help you build the body you've always yearned for without blowing up like the Pillsbury Doughboy.

Eat Real Food

To quote America's foremost food writer, Michael Pollan, "Don't eat anything your grandmother wouldn't recognize as food." Protein powders notwithstanding, this is great advice. Whole foods like lean meats, nuts, seeds, and vegetables contain more of the nutrients muscles crave, and deliver a steadier supply of amino acids and blood glucose to muscles than the nutritional dreck found in the middle aisles of your local supermarket.

Rise & Done

When trying to gain mass, eat two breakfasts. To restock liver glycogen and put the brakes on the catabolism that chips away at your muscle overnight, down two scoops of whey protein along with a fast-digesting carb such as Vitargo or white bread immediately upon waking. One of our favorite morning shakes is two cups of coffee, two scoops of whey, and two to three tablespoons of sugar. About 60 minutes later, follow up with a whole foods breakfast that boasts quality protein—such as Canadian bacon or eggs—and slower burning carbs, such as oatmeal

Track Your Intake

The only way you'll know if you're eating enough in the right proportions to grow muscle is to keep a detailed food diary, and tally your calories and macronutrients. The huge database of foods at nutritiondata.com can help you crunch the numbers.

Get Your Game On

Game meat used to be a big part of the American dinner—bring it back. Bison, elk, ostrich, and venison are among the best muscle-building foods. Besides having a superior protein-tofat ratio that helps pack on lean mass, most game is grass fed and has plenty of room to roam. This produces more fat-burning omega-3s and conjugated linoleic acid. Look for game meat at farmers' markets or order at eatwild.com. Also, keep an eye out for game meat jerky, a stellar, protein-packed snack option

Eat Whey Protein Before and After Workouts

In a study published in the journal Amino Acids, Finnish scientists discovered that weightlifters who consumed whey protein before and immediately after workouts produced more of a compound called cyclin-dependent kinase 2, or CDK2, than those who didn't take whey. CDK2 is believed to activate muscle stem cells involved in hypertrophy and recovery from intense training. In addition, a 2009 study by Japanese researchers found that consuming whey and glucose prompted larger stores of posttraining muscle glycogen (the main energy source for working muscles) than ingesting just glucose. Shoot for 20–30 grams of fast-digesting whey protein isolate or hydrolysate 30 minutes pre-workout and immediately post-workout.

Don't Shun Carbs

To gain mass, you must eat plenty of carbohydrates: two to three grams per pound of body weight. Carbs contain the calories required for growth, and glycogen to fuel intense lifting. Good options for most meals are brown rice, oatmeal, quinoa, and sweet potatoes. However, in your first meal of the day and your post-workout snack—when an insulin spike is needed to channel amino acids into muscles—you want fastdigesting carbs such as fruit, white potatoes, or white rice.

Plan Ahead

Coming home ravenous after a ballsout training session and having nothing ready to eat can send you on a hunt for the nearest bag of Doritos. But having a stockpile of protein-packed foods that can be reheated easily guarantees you'll make healthy choices and get the nutrients your muscles need. Use the weekend to rustle up big batches of chicken, chili, stews, hard-boiled eggs, and rice, which will keep in the fridge or freezer the whole week.

Munch Before Bed

Before hitting the sack, snack on a combination of slow-digesting casein protein and healthy fat. Casein coagulates in the gut, ensuring a steady supply of amino acids to slow catabolism as you sleep. About 30 minutes before bedtime, have 20–40 grams of casein protein powder or one cup of unsweetened low-fat cottage cheese (a stellar casein source) mixed with two tablespoons of flaxseed oil or one to two ounces of nuts or seeds.

Schedule Frequent Noshing

Eating often will keep you satiated and give your muscles the constant stream of nutrients they need to grow. Not only are hunger pangs a sign that your body may have entered a catabolic state, but when you're starving you're more likely to OD on leftover birthday cake at the office. Try to consume eight physique-friendly meals or snacks throughout the day, including your pre- and post-workout fare.

Wolf Down Enough Calories

Muscle, unlike flab, is a metabolically active tissue, and you need to put away plenty of calories to keep it growing. Eat too few calories and you'll whittle it away. When mass gain is the goal, aim to consume about 20 calories per pound of body weight each day (about 3,600 calories for a 180-pound guy). If you find that 20 calories per pound packs on mass and fat, drop to 16–18 calories. But this doesn't mean you've got the green light to pound pizza. Quality matters too, so keep it clean.

Face the Facts

Fat, including the much-maligned saturated fat, is necessary for building a rock-solid physique. It revs up testosterone production, provides necessary calories, and helps your joints endure the heavy lifting needed to spur muscle gains. Aim for at least 0.5 grams of fat per pound of body weight (90 grams for a 180-pound man), or 30% of your total daily calories. Divide that into equal thirds from saturated fats found in beef, coconut products, and dairy; monounsaturated fats from almonds, avocado, olive oil, and peanut butter; and fat-burning polyunsaturated fats found in fatty fish, flaxseeds, hemp seeds, and walnuts. Avoid the trans-fatty acids found in fried foods.

Pack in Protein

Protein provides the amino acids used to build muscle. Shoot for 1–1.5 grams of protein per pound of body weight, or 180–270 grams a day for a 180-pounder. Top protein picks include dairy, eggs, poultry, red meat, and seafood. These foods offer a wealth of complete protein, providing your muscles with the aminos necessary for recovery and growth. You may supplement with whey, casein, and soy protein powders as well. And don't overlook plant-based protein sources such as quinoa, beans, and hemp seeds.

Mass-Gain Meal Plan

BREAKFAST 1
2 scoops whey protein
2 cups coffee
2–3 tbsp sugar

BREAKFAST 2
3 large eggs
2 cups oatmeal

MIDMORNING SNACK
8 oz plain 2% Greek yogurt

½ cup blueberries
¼ cup walnuts

LUNCH
6 oz. bison sirloin steak
2 medium wholewheat tortillas
½ cup salsa
2 cups multicolored green salad
1 tbsp oil and vinegar dressing

PRE-WORKOUT
1 scoop whey protein
1 scoop casein protein
1 cup cherries
12 oz water

POST-WORKOUT
1 scoop whey protein
1 scoop casein protein
1 cup fat-free milk
2 slices white bread
1 tbsp jelly

DINNER
6 oz rainbow trout
1½ cups quinoa
1 cup broccoli

BEDTIME SNACK
1 cup 1% cottage cheese
2 tsp flaxseed oil

DAILY TOTALS
3,745 calories
341g protein

368g carbs
109g fat

NOTE: Mix all protein powders according to directions on label.

Eat Yourself Huge

To gain big-time mass

Truth be told, with 20 years of experience and a solid university background, even I lack the ability to peer into some sort of dietary crystal ball and devise an eating plan that promises nonstop results. Problem is, the body is always changing, and what works straight out of the gate for a few weeks may end up causing you to gain **unwanted body fat** thereafter. The only way to truly put together a **mass-gaining plan** that works is not to rigidly plan anything, but rather to continually re-evaluate yourself to ensure that what you're actually gaining is muscle, not body fat. Indeed, trial and error is your best bet.

That's the type of strategy Jay has always used. From the time he won the Teenage Nationals 15 years ago to his more recent victories, he has always been one to analyze, "Am I gaining muscle or fat?" It's the million-dollar question for many, and one I'll clear up for you right here and now.

Be Realistic

Bottom line, as long as you're gaining more muscle than body fat, you're headed in the right direction. That's important, because many are under the impression that it's possible to gain 100% pure fat-free muscle. Good luck.

In the real world, you'll always add some body fat with muscle, and that's okay. Here's why: Think about body composition, your muscle: fat ratio. If you gain 1 pound of fat and 2 pounds of muscle, you've actually become leaner. Yet if you add 3 pounds of fat over six weeks without adding muscle along with it, you're going in the wrong direction. But if you gained 3 pounds of muscle with that 3 pounds of fat, you're even. Now, if you gain 4, 5 or even 6 pounds of muscle with that 3 pounds of fat, you'll likely appear both bigger, since you've added muscle, and leaner, since you added more muscle than bodyfat. In this case, your muscle: fat ratio has shifted to the positive, the ultimate goal in any mass-gain diet.

The Markers

What to eat is important, but before mapping out a diet plan, you must know how to measure your progress so you can decide one of two things along the way: 1) whether to stay the course because you are, in fact, adding more muscle than body fat, or 2) switch gears because you're adding equal amounts of fat and muscle, or worse, more fat than muscle.

Here's where two tools come into play. The first is the bathroom scale. If you're lean, you should see the numbers increase. If they don't, you aren't eating enough protein and calories to push up your muscle weight. The second tool is a skin caliper to measure your body fat percentage. This will tell you how much of your weight is fat and how much is muscle mass. What you're looking for here is a decreasing body fat percentage, even if only slightly; any change in the negative direction is promising. Don't try to use the caliper by yourself or have just anyone take your measurements; you'll need to find a professional, either at your gym or in another health and wellness-type setting, who has experience administering such body fat tests.

Use both the scale and caliper before starting your mass-gaining diet to establish a starting point, then continue to use them on a weekly basis to chart your progress, or lack thereof, and make changes to your diet where necessary.

If your weight on the scale is increasing and your bodyfat percentage is decreasing, you're gaining muscle mass vs. fat. Stay the course and continue to do what you're doing diet-wise. If you're gaining considerably more muscle than fat, consider eating even more. If, on the other hand, you're gaining more fat than muscle, you'll have to make an adjustment immediately. Chances are you're eating too many carbs; more on that in a moment.

The Evaluation

So how does a guy like Jay do it? With 15 years of contest dieting under his belt, he'll jump on the scale and if it goes up, he'll continue doing what he's doing. If it doesn't go up, he'll increase his carbs and, to a lesser degree, his protein consumption. Bodyfat and skin calipers? This pro doesn't need 'em. He has enough experience to look in the mirror and determine if he's adding fat or not. But then again, he was Mr. Olympia and you weren't. So stick with a skinfold caliper (at least for now) to pinpoint your bodyfat level.

After you step on the scale and have your bodyfat percentage measured, follow the simple dietary guidelines listed earlier and train as you normally would (assuming you hit the gym regularly). Do this for 2-3 weeks, then retake your bodyweight and bodyfat measurements. Write down these numbers and, depending on your scenario, proceed as follows.

- **Scenario 1:** If the number on the scale is higher and there's no change in bodyfat percentage via skinfold caliper measurements - in other words, you're adding size and holding steady in terms of leanness - continue using our simplified dietary guidelines.

- **Scenario 2:** If the scale isn't budging at all, you're not eating enough. Try doubling up on carbs at two meals other than the postworkout meal. Consider adding more protein as well by eating, for example, 9 or 10 ounces of meat instead of 6 ounces at two meals other than the postworkout meal.

- **Scenario 3:** If your bodyweight has increased and you find via the caliper that you're adding equal amounts of muscle and fat, decrease your intake of carbs. Eliminate them at any two meals, preferably the final two meals of the day. (You'll use more carbs earlier in the day; carbs consumed at night are more likely to be stored as bodyfat.) If you train at night, however, you'll still need the larger postworkout meal; in that case, eliminate carbohydrates at two meals besides postworkout.

- **Scenario 4:** If the number on the scale is increasing and you're losing bodyfat, double your carb intake at all meals and start eating 1 1/2 times the original protein suggestions at each meal. In other words, push the envelope. Your body's not gaining fat, so eat as much as you can. The reason behind the fat loss is typically a metabolism increase - calorie-burning - that can accompany a gain in mass.

- **Scenario 5:** You were seeing great results for, say, four weeks, with an increase in bodyweight without adding bodyfat. Then, wham - your bodyfat shoots up from 10% to 12%. The solution: Reduce carbs at your two final meals of the day. If you're eating two potatoes, go to one; if you're eating one potato, cut it in half. Stick with this for a couple of weeks and your bodyfat levels should come back down. Then you can increase your carbs again, and this time around, your body may add muscle with little or no bodyfat.

The point is, no one really knows how your body will react and respond, which is why you have to continually measure your progress and change your diet accordingly. Come to think of it, the best person to devise a mass-gain diet for you is you.

The Diet Basics

In this diet, you'll set aside all mathematical calculations - there's no recording every last gram of carbs, protein and fat or counting calories. Instead, keep it simple:

Start off eating seven meals a day, with carbs and protein at each meal. Protein-wise, you'll need to consume roughly 1.5-2 grams of protein per pound of bodyweight per day. Eat one of the following protein sources at each meal (based on a 160-200-pound individual).

- 6 ounces chicken breast
- 6 ounces deli turkey
- 7 ounces lean ground beef
- 6 ounces canned tuna
- 4 whole eggs and 4 egg whites
- 1 1/2 cups fat-free cottage cheese
- 2 scoops whey protein powder (mixed in water)

As for carbs, keep them coming all day, spread more or less evenly over six meals. Pick one of the following at each meal:

- 1 large sweet potato
- 1 large potato
- 2 cups cooked oatmeal
- 1 cup cooked rice
- 3 slices whole-wheat bread
- 1 cup cooked pasta

Each meal will be a combination of one serving of protein that nets you about 40 grams and one serving of a carbohydrate source that gives you about 40-50 grams, as listed above. For example, for dinner you might have a 6-ounce chicken breast with a large sweet potato or a cup of rice. The only exception is your immediate postworkout meal. Here, you'll double up on carbs, so instead of 1 cup of rice, you'll have 2 cups. The reason for the larger post-training meal is that the body needs the additional protein and carbs to kick-start muscle recovery, growth and repair. If you eat too little here, you shortchange your progress. And don't turn away from every form of fat. Healthy fats, such as those in eggs, avocadoes, nuts and fatty fish, will help you stay lean, recover from workouts and put on quality muscle mass.

Massive Meal Plan

Here's a basic plan to get the 160-200-pounder started. You can switch the foods around to various meals depending on your personal preferences, but this should serve as the basis of your mass-gaining diet. Every week or so, step on the scale and get your bodyfat measured by a professional. Then alter your portion sizes accordingly, based on the "quick fixes" guidelines below.

Meal 1 - Breakfast
4 whole eggs and 4 egg whites 1,3
2 cups cooked oatmeal 1,2

Meal 2 - Snack
6 oz. canned tuna 3
3 slices whole-wheat bread 3
1 Tbsp. fat-free mayo

Meal 3 - Lunch
7 oz. lean ground beef 3
1 cup cooked pasta
1/4 cup spaghetti sauce
1 cup sliced zucchini

Meal 4 - Preworkout
2 scoops whey protein powder with water 3
2 cups cooked oatmeal 3

Meal 5 - Postworkout
2 scoops whey protein powder with water 1,3
1 cup rice 1,3

Meal 6 - Dinner
6 oz. chicken breast 3
1 large sweet potato 2,4
1 cup broccoli

Meal 7 - Bedtime
1/2 cups fat-free cottage cheese 3
1 cup cooked pasta 2,4
1/4 cup spaghetti sauce

DAILY TOTALS: 3,769 calories, 363 g protein, 433 g carbs, 69 g fat

QUICK FIXES

1 Scenario 2: You're not gaining weight. Eat twice the amount of carbs and 1.5 times as much protein at two of your meals during the day.

2 Scenario 3: You're gaining weight, but it's as much fat as it is muscle. Eliminate carbs at your last two meals of the day, excluding your postworkout meal.

3 Scenario 4: You're gaining weight and losing bodyfat. Follow the directions in Scenario 2 above at every meal.

4 Scenario 5: You did fine at first, but now your bodyfat has increased. Halve your carbs at your final two meals. If your bodyfat falls in two weeks, increase your carbs.

Get Big on Pig

Try this protein-packed pork tenderloin.

Sweet, spicy, and full of muscle-building protein, this pork tenderloin with bell pepper marmalade dish makes it easy for you to get whole-food protein in a variety of convenient ways. If you're watching your carbs, eat it straight of the plate. For times when you aren't as carb conscious, portion it out over garlic bread, which is my personal favorite and described in the instructions below. It also makes a great topper for nachos or taco filling. No matter what your preference, it's hard to go wrong with these.

Calories:

305

Protein:

34g

Fat:

9g

Carbs:

Optimized Nutrition Volume, 3: **building big biceps**

19g

Cook time:

45-60 minutes

Servings:

12 appetizer portions

Ingredients:

2 tbsp

Grapeseed oil

3 lbs.

Tenderloin

1/4 - 1/2 cup

Roaster Garlic Pepper

1

Red Onion (diced)

1

Red Bell Pepper (diced)

1

Orange Bell Pepper (diced)

Optimized Nutrition Volume, 3: **building big biceps**

1/2 cup

Honey

1/2 cup

Red Wine Vinegar

2 tbsp

Tabasco Sauce

1/2 cup

Cranberry Sauce

For Garlic Bread: 4 tbsp.

Butter

2 oz.

Extra virgin olive oil

4 cloves

Garlic (minced)

1

Baguette (cut into 1/2 inch slices)

Equipment:
- Kitchen knife

- Cutting board
- Large saute pan
- Roasting pan
- Skillet

Instructions:

1. 1) Preheat oven to 350 degrees.
2. 2) Heat grapeseed oil in large sauté pan and sear pork on all sides.
3. 3) Transfer pork to roasting pan, rub with garlic pepper, and roast in oven until tender, 45–60 minutes. Allow pork to rest 8–10 minutes before slicing.
4. 4) While pork is in oven, heat onions and peppers in hot skillet (dry, no oil) for 3 minutes—removing liquid by "sweating them down."
5. 5) Add honey, vinegar, wine, hot sauce, and cranberry sauce. Stir well. Reduce over medium-low heat until no liquid remains and marmalade is thick.
6. 6) Slice pork and assemble appetizers by layering a pork medallion and a small amount of marmalade on garlic bread. You can also enjoy as dip, entrée, or sandwich.
7. For the garlic bread: Melt butter in olive oil over low heat. Add garlic and cook until soft. Assemble bread slices on baking sheet and spoon garlic mixture onto each. Lightly toast bread in oven while pork sits.
8. Each slice of garlic bread adds 18g carbs, 7g fat and 4g of protein.

How Much Protein, Carbohydrate and Fat Do You Need?

Normally, when you think about building muscle, you think protein. But that shouldn't be the only thing on your plate.

Q: I'm trying to put together the best possible mass-gaining meal plan. Where should I start?

A: Normally, when you think about **building muscle**, you think protein. But Mike Francois, past winner of the Arnold Classic, knows that shouldn't be the only thing on your plate. Mass-building requires energy, through high carbohydrate intake. "To **gain mass**, you have to ensure you're getting enough protein to rebuild muscle tissue damaged through training, but you also have to eat a lot of carbohydrates because gaining size requires you to fill your muscles with glycogen," he says.

Glycogen is the collection of carbohydrates stored in muscles that powers your training and affects anabolism; think of it as an energy stockpile. To maintain that supply as you're trying to gain muscle, you need a slight positive intake in carbohydrates at each meal -- that is, you have to eat more carbohydrates than you burn.

What does Mike consider an ideal meal? "For someone who is training hard and weighs over 200 pounds, I'd suggest 6-8 ounces of chicken breast, 2 cups of brown rice, a tablespoon of olive oil and a cup of broccoli. That provides 109 grams of carbohydrates, about 60 grams of protein and 24 grams of fat."

Mike doesn't beat up on dietary fat: "**Unsaturated fats, especially olive oil, are essential**. They help all kinds of functions in the body that affect growth. Plus, they're a dense source of calories, which is an important factor in adding weight."

Vegetables are another must. "People think they're a diet food, but they're important because of their fiber content." Fiber helps cleanse the intestines, and some speculate this can increase nutrient absorption, yet another consideration in growth and tissue repair.

Finding a Balance

Celebrity trainer David "Scooter" Honig helps chisel the physiques of luminaries, including pop star LL Cool J and WBA World Boxing Champion Vivian "Vicious" Harris. He describes the ideal pre-training combo he uses with Harris: "I have Vivian eat scrambled egg whites mixed with a whole egg or 20-30 grams of protein powder from whey because it gets in the system quickly and doesn't upset his stomach. Energywise, he sticks with a cup of oatmeal for the opposite reason: It digests slower, giving him sustained energy for his workout."

Honig also acknowledges that the ideal meal can change from person to person, depending on metabolism. "I try to monitor my client's bodyfat and energy levels," he says. "If Vivian is low on energy, the ideal meal remains the same in terms of what to eat, but the quantities change; in that case, we'd boost the carbs. On the other hand, if his bodyweight is going up, say he's gaining fat, the carb portion has to come down."

That's the tricky part of establishing a meal plan. The ideal meal contains ideal nutrients: lean proteins, complex carbohydrates for energy and glycogen replenishment, moderate amounts of dietary fat, plus veggies for fiber. What changes is the quantity. If you weigh more than 200 pounds, you need at least 40-55 grams of protein per meal. If you're in the 150-190 range, that could come down to 30-35 grams. Carbohydrate amounts vary even more based on individual bodyweight, bodyfat and metabolism. One easy approach: If you weigh more than 200 pounds, fix your carbs at 80-100 grams per meal. If you weigh 190 or less, set them at 60-80 per meal. Success will come with figuring out what works best for your body.

12 Surefire Muscle-Building Nutrition Tips

Maximize your muscle with this list of dietary maxims.

You know that **protein** builds muscle. Duh. You know that you want to avoid fast-burning carbs if your aim is to **stay lean**, and you know that you should be drinking lots of water a day—a gallon or more if you're active. If you're reading this odds are good you have more than a passing interest in such matters, so we'll dispense with the basics.

The following compilation of sound nutritional tips is for those who already know the difference between carbs, fat and protein and who are looking for a dietary edge that will help them to maximize their muscle gains. That, we're guessing, is you.

1. EAT BOTH FATTY AND LOW-FAT FISH

Fish is an excellent source of protein that should be consumed regularly by bodybuilders. Varying in fat content, some types of fish are high in healthy fats while others are low in fat altogether. Unlike other tissue proteins, though, fatty fish provide a host of benefits to bodybuilders.

Salmon and sardines, for example, are excellent sources of omega-3 fatty acids, which support the immune system and assist with muscle recovery and growth, in addition to many other benefits. Fish that are lower in fat, such as tuna, also make an excellent source of protein. All bodybuilders, regardless of their phase of diet or training goals, should strive to take in eight ounces of fatty fish at least twice a week.

2. EAT YOUR VEGGIES!

Vegetables are one of the most overlooked components of bodybuilding nutrition. Many bodybuilders are rigorous about their protein and complex carbohydrate consumption, but lax about eating a sufficient quantity and variety of vegetables. Bodybuilders should strive to take in five or six servings every day.

To meet your needs, include more than one serving at a meal. Not only do vegetables provide nutrien

ts that other bodybuilding foods may lack, but they also provide bulk and fiber, helping your body more efficiently process a high-protein diet.

3. TAKE GLUTAMINE

Known for its immunity-enhancing properties, **glutamine** is not only one of the most prevalent aminos in the body, but also one of the most important for bodybuilders. If you're overly stressed from dieting or training, supplementing with glutamine allows your body to maintain its storage supply of glutamine in muscle tissue, enhancing overall muscular growth and recovery. Take 10-40 g of glutamine a day.

4. MIX YOUR ANTIOXIDANTS

Take a mix of antioxidants; a good cocktail has an anticatabolic effect by quenching free radicals formed during and after intense exercise. In your antioxidant regimen include 400-800 international units (IU) of vitamin E, 500-1,000 milligrams (mg) of vitamin C, 200 micrograms of selenium (from selenium yeast). Get the rest from five or six servings of fruits and vegetables per day.

5. ADD ARGININE

Try adding **arginine** to your supplement mix. Arginine, a conditionally essential amino acid, seems promising in the muscle-building department, although not by aiding growth-hormone release, as previously believed. Studies suggest it speeds wound healing, which isn't too far removed from what happens in the body after a workout.

Arginine also improves blood flow and enhances the growth of muscles lengthwise (new contractile units are built onto muscle at a faster rate when arginine is given to developing rats). Arginine may also enhance immune function in athletes, especially when combined with glutamine.

6. MAXIMIZE YOUR MINERALS

Take extra calcium and magnesium. If you look at the label of any once-daily multivitamin, you'll notice a "mineral gap"—a place where certain minerals should be listed. Even if they're included, most multis contain only a small percentage of the Daily Value (% DV) of calcium, magnesium and potassium.

Calcium is important for fat-burning metabolism, magnesium for training performance and potassium for muscle cell volume. A once-daily multivitamin simply doesn't cut it. Correct the situation by taking 1,000 mg per day of supplement-source calcium (or two to three cups of fat-free dairy products), 450 mg of magnesium, and five or six servings of fruits and vegetables per day (for potassium as well as other micronutrients).

7. TRY TYROSINE

Give the amino acid **tyrosine** a try to prevent burnout caused by lack of sleep, stress and/or use of thermogenic supplements. Taking 1-4 g of it early in the day is recommended. In studies using military personnel as subjects, tyrosine was shown to increase performance under stress. It is a precursor to fat-burning hormones that stimulate norepinephrine.

8. TAKE ZMA

ZMA is a specifically formulated combination of zinc and magnesium. The benefits of ZMA supplementation include improved recovery due to enhanced sleep efficiency and increased anabolic hormone levels, as well as greater gains in muscle strength and power. For best results, take ZMA on an empty stomach before bedtime. Follow label recommendations for dosage.

10. DON'T SKIP THE VITAMIN C

Vitamin C is a powerful antioxidant that helps in the synthesis of hormones, amino acids and collagen. It also protects immune-system cells from damage and allows them to work more efficiently. The body cannot store vitamin C, so it must be frequently supplemented. Multivitamins contain C, but additional supplementation will ensure that you don't have a deficit. Take 500-1,000 mg per day.

10. BOOST PROTEIN BEFORE BEDTIME

One of the best ways to prevent your body from tapping into muscle stores for energy is to take in a moderate amount of protein shortly before going to bed at night. Thirty to fifty grams of protein, consumed before going to sleep, will provide your body with the nutrients it needs to repair and build muscles. A protein shake is ideal before bedtime. Lean meats, nuts and seeds are reasonable alternatives.

11. CYCLE BETWEEN HIGH- AND LOW-CARB DAYS

One excellent way to keep your metabolic rate up and your body burning fat is to change the amount of carbohydrates you eat on a daily basis. Eating high carbs all the time allows your body to readily store them as bodyfat. Eating low carbs all the time encourages your body to tear down muscle tissue for energy. To get the best of both worlds—keeping your muscle while avoiding bodyfat—schedule a higher-carb day after every three to five low-carb days.

12. USE CHEAT FOODS AS PART OF YOUR DIET STRATEGY

On the surface, this may seem to contradict the previous point, but when implemented properly, it doesn't. The mindless consumption of junk and processed foods destroys bodybuilding progress faster than almost anything else does, Judicious selection of a cheat food, however, can help keep you sane and help ensure your adherence to your overall diet strategy.

Cut out junk food that you don't crave. If you have a craving, feed the beast, but keep it moderate. If doughnuts are your thing, allow yourself that Sunday morning Krispy Kreme. Have a slice of pizza occasionally. Just set limits and adhere to them.

5 Things You Should Know About Avocados

Think you know everything about this super food? Think again!

1) A whole, medium-size avocado (about fiveounces) has 226 caloriesand contains about three grams of protein and nine grams of fiber.

2) More than 80% of an avocado's calories comes from fat, most of which are healthy, monounsaturated fats. One of those fats—oleic acid—has been shown to reduce cholesterol levels.

3) While the banana is most famous for potassium content, a typical avocado contains 35% more potassium (684 milligrams vs. 505) than that of its long, yellow cousin. Avocados are also a decent source of calcium and magnesium, crucial electrolytes for athletes because of their role in muscle function and fluid balance.

4) Every avocado contains nearly 20 vitamins, minerals, and phytonutrients—nutrients derived from plant material that provide a defense against cancers, heart disease, and signs of premature aging.

5) Regular consumption of healthy fats like the ones found in avocados has been shown to promote a boost in testosterone and growth hormone production.

5 Things You Should Know About Eggs

Get the low down on this muscle-building staple

1| Rocky didn't know what the hell he was doing. Besides the salmonella risk, downing eggs raw won't provide as much fuel for muscle growth. Studies show that the protein in fully cooked eggs is 91% bio available, or ready to be used by the body. Raw eggs are only half as potent.

2| While a yolk carries all of an egg's five grams of fat and 186 mg of cholesterol, it also packs about half the egg's six grams of protein, as well as its payload of amino acids and vitamins A, B, D, E, and K. This is why many lifters opt for whole eggs plus added whites.

3| Egg yolks contain choline, an essential nutrient that helps maintain brain-cell structure and neurotransmitters./p>

4| The spindly white fiber attached to the yolk is called the chalaza, which protects the yolk by keeping it suspended within the shell.

5| There is absolutely no nutritional difference between brown eggs and white ones. Brown eggs are laid by hens with red earlobes, and white eggs are laid by hens with white earlobes. End of story.

5 Things You Need to Know About Oatmeal

Get the breakdown on this highly recommended pre-workout food.

1. Oatmeal *comes in several varieties*

Steel-cut oats are chopped oat groats and are the least processed; rolled (or old-fashioned) oats are steamed and rolled flat; instant oats are precooked and dried, and often contain added sugar.

2. Slow-digesting *carbs offer long-lasting energy when eaten before workouts*

Blend 1/2 cup rolled oats, 1 scoop whey protein and 1 1/2 cups water to make an easy all-in-one pre-workout shake.

3. One serving offers an array of macros

(1/2 cup) of cooked steel-cut oats has 150 calories, 5 g protein, 27 g carbs, 2 g fat and 4 g fiber. One serving (1 cup) of cooked rolled oats has an extra gram of fat. One packet of plain instant oats has 100 calories, 4 g protein, 19 g carbs, 2 g fat and 3 g fiber.

4. You can cook *steel-cut oats quickly*

In a large microwave-safe bowl combine 1/2 cup steel-cut oats, 1/2 cup 1% milk and 1/2 cup water. Microwave for four minutes, stir and cook for two more minutes.

5. You can substitute *oats for bread crumbs in just about any recipe*

Finely chop oats with a knife or food processor, then add them to ground beef to make meatballs or meatloaf, or use them to bread fish or chicken fillets.

Section 4 : SUPPLEMENT STACK

Optimized Nutrition Volume, 3: building big biceps

If you don't know the difference between whey protein and casein protein, you might be a first-time supplement user. If you think NO is an effective way to tell your kid or dog to stop what he's doing, you might be a first-time supplement user. If you're reading this article, you might be a first-time supplement user.

Don't worry - being considered a first-time supplement user isn't as demeaning as being considered a redneck. In fact, we're glad you finally recognized the benefits that supplements provide as you pursue your bodybuilding goals. Allow us to walk you through the basics of supplement science to give you the know-how to build your first stack. You'll be an expert in no time, armed with the knowledge to create more advanced stacks as you progress in ability and experience. The following seven supplements are all you'll need to add mass, maintain energy and stay healthy.

Arginine
Arginine is an amino acid that's readily converted to nitric oxide (NO) in the body. NO is involved in many physical processes, but the most vital to you is vasodilation, which is the process that increases blood flow to muscles, allowing better delivery of nutrients and oxygen. Arginine can boost growth hormone levels as well. Dose: Take 3-5 grams on an empty stomach in the morning, before workouts and before bed.

Creatine
We'll keep it short since you can read everything you need to know about creatine on pages 128-129. Creatine is an amino acid-like supplement that provides the quick energy you need for powerful muscle contractions, such as when lifting weights. It also allows your muscles to hold more water, making them fuller and stronger, which ultimately stimulates additional growth.
Dose: Take 3-5 grams before and after workouts.

HMB
One of the best supplements for true beginners is beta-hydroxy-beta-methylbutyrate (HMB). It's a metabolite of leucine, the most essential of the branched-chain amino acids (BCAAs); however, it's considered to be a more effective form of leucine. Supplementing with HMB prevents muscle breakdown, encourages muscle growth and aids fat-burning processes in the body. Research shows it's very effective at increasing muscle mass and strength in beginner-level trainees, but it may be less effective in more experienced lifters.
Dose: Take 1-3 grams with food in the morning, before and after workouts, and before bed.

Whey Protein
If there's one supplement every bodybuilder needs - regardless of experience - it's whey protein powder. Taken before and after workouts, this fast-digesting protein provides the amino acids required to build muscle protein at the most critical time for growth. Whey is a good source of the BCAAs leucine, isoleucine and valine. Leucine, a key stimulator of protein synthesis, starts the processes for building muscle protein and uses the other aminos as the building blocks for making more. Dose: Take 20 grams before workouts and another 20-40 grams after workouts.

Glutamine
Glutamine happens to be one of the most plentiful amino acids found in the human body. Not only is it crucial for recovery and muscle growth, but it also buffers the fatigue-inducing chemicals that form during intense exercise. By delaying fatigue, you can bang out more reps. In addition, glutamine is essential for normal digestion and immune

function. Supplementing with it protects your muscles from being broken down for fuel by your body to access the stored glutamine.
Dose: Start with 2-3 grams and work up slowly to 5 grams, taken in the morning, before and after workouts and before bed.

Multivitamin/Mineral
Whatever your level of training experience, you must take a multivitamin/mineral supplement. It may not sound sexy, but building muscle requires adequate amounts of vitamins and minerals to do the work. Even if you eat a healthful diet, you still need to take a multi because vitamin and mineral contents of many foods have declined significantly due to modern farming practices. In addition, hard training depletes stores of certain vitamins and minerals. Choose one that contains the full spectrum of vitamins and minerals and provides 100% of the daily value (DV) of most of these.
Dose: Take one dose with food twice a day. You may also want to consider taking some extra B vitamins, such as a B complex, as well as the antioxidant vitamins C and E. The B vitamins are important for proper protein and fat metabolism, while vitamins C and E scavenge free radicals, protecting your muscles and the rest of your body from cellular damage. Try a B complex that provides 50 mg of B1 and B6, and 50 mcg of B12. Take 500-1,000 mg of Vitamin C twice a day, and 400-800 IU of Vitamin E once daily, both with food.

Fish Oil
Fish oil supplements containing the essential omega-3 fatty acids eicosapentaenoic acid (EPA) and docosahexaenoic acid (DHA) reduce the risk of heart disease and stroke, prevent muscle breakdown, help regenerate and grow muscle, enhance joint tissue rebuilding and encourage fat loss. Eating fatty fish like salmon several times a week may provide all the omega-3s you need, but concerns about the levels of mercury and PCBs (a mixture of individual chemicals found in the environment that are related to several health problems) in fish have caused many people to cut back on their fish intake. The good news is that a recent study found no traces of either in more than 40 brands of fish oil supplements.
Dose: Each day, take 2-6 grams in two divided doses with food. M&F

TALE OF TWO STACKS
Just because you may be a supplement beginner doesn't mean you're a beginner in the gym. These two first-time stacks are designed with your lifting experience in mind.

Old-Timer Stack
Why did you wait so long to give supplements a try? Whatever your reason, here you are with significant lifting experience but a lack of supplement savvy. This stack includes whey protein, a multivitamin/mineral, fish oil, creatine, glutamine and arginine. The only thing missing is HMB. Most research supports the effectiveness of HMB in beginning lifters, but the gains seem to be less impressive with experienced trainees. However, some anecdotal evidence suggests that when HMB is taken in higher doses (3-5 grams in the morning, before and after workouts and before bed), it's very effective even in highly trained lifters. We suggest sticking with this stack for a couple of months before adding HMB so you can better gauge how effective it is for you.

Supplement	Dose
Whey Protein	20 g preworkout 20-40 g postworkout
Creatine	3-5 g pre- and postworkout
Arginine	3-5 g morning, preworkout and before bed

Optimized Nutrition Volume, 3: building big biceps

Supplement	Dose
Glutamine	2-3 g* in the morning, pre- and postworkout and before bed
Multivitamin/mineral	1 dose with breakfast and dinner
Fish Oil	1-3 g with breakfast and lunch

* Work up to 5 g over several weeks.

The Green Stack

For those of you just beginning a lifting program who want to start stacking supplements right away, this one is for you. It includes HMB, a supplement found to be very effective in beginner lifters, as well as a multivitamin/ mineral, whey protein and arginine.

The most surprising part of this stack may be what's not included: Creatine isn't present because you'll make significant gains in your first six months of training anyway; use it when your gains have slowed and you want a boost in size and strength. You won't find glutamine, either, because your training intensity likely isn't high enough to deplete your muscles of this critical amino acid. Nor will you take fish oil at this time: While it protects joints and enhances their healing, as well as prevents muscle breakdown, you're probably not lifting heavy enough yet to warrant its use.

Supplement	Dose
Whey Protein	20 g preworkout 20-40 g postworkout
Arginine	3-5 g morning, preworkout and before bed
HMB	1-3 g with food in the morning, pre- and postworkout and before bed
Multivitamin/ mineral	1 dose with breakfast and dinner

Optimized Nutrition Volume, 3: building big biceps

Joint Relief Supplement Stack

This supplement stack may not sound very excited by the name but you may find a few of the supplements within this stack to be a necessity at times. If you've been lifting weights for a while then more than likely you have already, or will at some point experience sore joints. Joint pain is strange as in you may have shoulder pain for a few weeks and then knee pain for another few weeks. For me, joint pain has come and gone but I've found that if I start taking a reliable supplement that's proven to relieve sore joints the pain isn't as severe and it usually subsides quickly.

I'm going to highlight two supplements I take for joint relief. Since this is a **supplement stack**, I'm also going to list the rest of the supplements you can take that may not be relevant to relieving joint pain. These are supplements like pre and post workout supplements, multi-vitamins, protein powder, etc. My intent here is to create a well-rounded supplement stack, yet catered to joint relief.

First I'll go over the non-relevant supplements to joint pain I'm taking in this stack. These are supplements I normally take with any supplement regimen I'm on (BCAAs, creatine, etc). I'll also list the brands, though those usually change as I'm always trying new supplements. This will be followed by the two relevant supplements for sore joints.

Non-Relevant Supplements for Joint Relief
Whey Protein – Dymatize Elite

Multi-Vitamins – Optimum Nutrition Opti-Men

Pre Workout – Warrior Labz Amp3d

Intra Workout – Gaspari Nutrition Aminolast

Post Workout – Universal Nutrition Storm

Relevant Supplements for Joint Relief
Spring Valley Fish Oil

USPlabs SuperCissus

Fish oil is something I take consistently in my supplement regimen. There's a ton of health and heart benefits to taking fish oil, and fish oil is also known to soothe joint pain. The other, and probably the main highlight of this joint relief supplement stack is **SuperCissus by USPlabs**. This supplement contains the extract Cissus Quadrangularis. Cissus is said to support healthy muscles and bones, and delivers nutrients to the tendons.

This stack is a little different from many of the old supplements that contain glucosamine, choindroitin, and msm. I've personally never had any luck with those ingredients anyway. But I can attest to the combination of fish oil and cissus quadrangularis being extremely helpful to relieving my joint pain on more than one occasion. So if you're experiencing sore joints, try this stack.

Old School Supplement Stack

I'm turning back the clock to the late 80's and early 90's which is the era I started weight training. Back then we didn't have the vast array of supplements for bodybuilding and strength training. And I must admit the protein powders back then were less than desirable. I'm sure some of you remember those protein powders that didn't mix well and tasted like chalk! However, there was one supplement introduced that changed the entire industry of supplements, bodybuilding, and strength training forever. That supplement is creatine monohydrate, and that's what I'm covering in what I call my 'Old School Muscle Building Supplement Stack.'

I'm covering the essentials while throwing in creatine monohydrate in this supplement plan. This is a basic, inexpensive yet very effective supplement stack and somewhat mirrors my **Basic Supplement**

Stack.
1) Whey Protein

2) Multi Vitamin

3) Fish Oil

4) Creatine Monohydrate

I've heard a few supplement companies knock creatine monohydrate. And many supplement companies have produced other versions of creatine that's said to be more efficient. But I don't know if there's any more science and research on these other types of creatines as there is on creatine monohydrate. My philosophy is creatine monohydrate worked extremely well for a lot of people back then; it's not going to all of a sudden stop working, right? If it worked then, it still works now.

There are a small number of people that have claimed to not respond to creatine monohydrate. There are plenty of other supplements on the market geared towards building muscle if you're one of those people. I've personally never known anyone that didn't respond to this supplements.

I've experimented several methods of taking creatine monohydrate but these days I take it after my workout with my post workout shake (I train early mornings). I also sometimes take it later that day with my dinner. And I usually take about 7-10 grams each time. Some folks like to load creatine monohydrate for 5 days as instructed but I personally have never seen the benefit of that. Although it could work well for you.

I also threw in a very basic multi vitamin for the purpose of this Old School Muscle Building Stack to keep it simple. I do realize that Universal's Animal Pak was around and very popular back but for the supplement stack video below, I chose to use Optimum Nutrition's Opti-Men.

Basic Muscle Building Supplement Stack

You can easily spend half of your paycheck on bodybuilding and nutritional supplements if you're not careful. So I wanted to share one of the basic supplement stacks I've been using for the past few years now. My goal here is to show you how to put together a basic yet effective supplement plan that won't break the bank. In the basic supplement stack video you'll find below, I show you the actual supplements I'm taking at that time. Whereas I do try new supplements from various supplements companies, the types of supplements I take pretty much stay the same. The only difference you may see in my supplement stack from time to time is if I throw in a testosterone boosting supplement or a fat burner. I don't have any of those in this video though. Again, this is a basic (and cost-effective) supplement stack.

The main purpose of this basic supplement stack is to present to you a solid foundation of what supplements are effective, and have been proven over time to help with recovery and building muscle. As I stated above, you can spend a ton of money on supplements and there are plenty of supplements on the market with new one's constantly being advertised. I think this is great as I love to see innovation and researchers finding new supplements and mixtures that will help us reach our fitness goals. The downside to that is it's easy to feel overwhelmed with all of the supplements, the research and studies, and all of the information (and misinformation) that's out there. That's why it's good to revert back to the basics of what has already been proven to work and simplify things.

Here's a brief rundown of the supplements:

1) Whey Protein – For this supplement stack I'm using Dymatize Elite Whey Protein Isolate. Whey protein is probably the most important supplements to weight lifters and bodybuilders, whether professional, or recreational (like me).

2) Multi-Vitamin/Training Pack – In the video I'm showing you Universal Nutrition Animal Pak for my training pack. I believe us weight trainers need more than just a regular vitamin than normal people take. Our bodies, since we break them down so much, need those extras. But if you're on a budget, a multi-vitamin is a must, at least.

3) Pre Workout Supplement – I usually keep two pre workout supplements on deck to switch them out every few days so my body doesn't get used to one. But for this stack I'm taking Nutrex Hemo Rage Black, the ultra concentrated version. I train in the early mornings (I'm in there by 4:45 AM) so pre workout supplements are important for me. I need help with the energy and focus.

4) & 5) – BCAAs and Creatine Post Workout – I'm putting these together because there are many post workout formulas that contain both branched chain amino acids and creatine, as well as many other ingredients to help you recover and build muscle. But in this particular supplement stack I'm taking Dymatize Elite Recoup for my BCAAs and Universal Nutrition's Storm for my creatine supplement. Both supplements are loaded with other goodies and I've found these two to be an effective post workout combination.

6) Fish Oil – I started taking fish oil after reading about the numerous health benefits of fish oil and I also noticed my joint pains were going away.

Performance and Recovery Supplement Stack

This supplement stack I'm sharing with you consists of the types of supplements I take pretty much year-round. It's a basic stack yet it covers what I feel are the essentials for optimal performance and recovery. You need that edge for performance to train with intensity. More importantly, you need supplements that help you recover in order to rebuild muscle tissue, lose body fat, and function at optimal levels, which in turn enhances your performance as well. For this supplement stack I'll give you specific supplements I'm using.

Supplements for Performance and Recovery

Type of Supplement	When	Supplement Brand
Whey Protein	post workout, between meals	Dymatize Elite Whey
Multi-Vitamin	twice a day with meals	Controlled Labs Orange Triad
Pre Workout	before workout	MusclePharm Assault
Post BCAAs	immediate post workout	Dymatize Elite Recoup
Post Workout Creatine	immediate post workout	ISS Complete Creatine Power
Fish Oil	twice a day with meals	Kirkland's Fish Oil

A high quality multi-vitamin and whey protein are always my top priorities in my supplement stacks. If I were broke and could only afford the minimum, those would be my go-to supplements. And beyond that, I feel a high quality multi-vitamin is the most important (you can always get protein from whole food sources). I'm using Orange Triad from Controlled Labs and Dymatize Elite Whey Isolate (the all natural version). I'll admit I rely on pre workout supplements now. I've tried nothing, I've tried just caffeine, and I've tried coffee. But my workouts are always 100% better and more intense with a solid pre workout supplement. In this supplement stack I had just started using Assault from MusclePharm which works extremely well for me.

As I stated in the recovery is of utmost importance in any supplement stack, so I harp on recovery here. I usually take some sort of BCAA supplement with creatine monohydrate immediate post workout (I'll have my post workout shake about 30 minutes later). In this case I'm using Dymatize Elite Recoup for BCAAs, which is also loaded with B vitamins and contains glutamine; all great for recovery. And I'm mixing that with ISS Complete Creatine Monohydrate (made with Creapure).

Lastly, I'm taking fish oil, Kirkland's Omega-3 Fish Oil (this is the Costco brand). I must note that whey protein and multi-vitamins also lean towards recovery.

This is a solid performance and recovery supplement stack that will indeed grant results if you're training hard and your diet is on key. You don't have to necessarily use the exact same supplements I'm using for this stack. For example, you may respond better to another type of pre workout supplement such as Animal Rage from Universal or Jack3d from USPlabs. I'm digging the MusclePharm Assault so I definitely recommend trying that. But the point is to use these types of supplements at specific times for optimal recovery and performance.

Tried and True Basics

Among the massive amount of products there are some proven muscle building supplements that have been proven to work and should be the staple of any supplement program. There are many formulas on the market that contain these supplements and more, such as the array of pre and post workout formulas (there are also now intra workout formulas). Some of these are great products, and of course some aren't so great.

Whether you choose to go with a formula or take individual supplements, I've listed a few key supplements that you should make sure you're taking as these are supplements that have been proven to work. My goal here is to prevent you from wasting money on useless products and supplements that don't work. And if you're like me, you've wasted enough money already on supplements that don't work.

Supplements that Work
Whey Protein
We all know that your body needs protein to build muscle. Whey protein is a superior source of protein due to its amino acid profile, rate of absorption, and the fact that its pure protein (most whey products have less than 1% fat and carbs). For some, whey protein is considered more of a necessity rather than a supplement, and thrown in their normal grocery budget. Whey protein digests quickly making it perfect for just about anytime during the day, but especially for pre and post workout meals. You may also use whey protein for snacks and in between meals.

Creatine
Creatine is a compound that delivers energy to your muscles and is one of the few proven supplements to produce results in building muscle, strength and improving performance. Creatine

still remains today one of the most popular muscle building supplements on the market. There are now numerous forms of creatine as supplement companies and constantly looking for the best path of absorption. However, the most common form of creatine is creatine monohydrate. This form usually works best when mixed with a non-acidic carbohydrate source as the release of insulin enhances the uptake of creatine.

Branched Chain Amino Acids (BCAAs)
Branched-chain amino acids consist of the three essential amino acids leucine, isoleucine, and valine. The body will breakdown muscle to use BCAAs for energy. This is why BCCAs are taken during and post workout to prevent muscle breakdown. BCAAs are another proven muscle building supplement.

Glutamine
Glutamine is a nonessential amino acid that plays an important role in muscle metabolism and repairing muscle tissue. Glutamine is often taken post workouts and before bed, although some studies show that it can be beneficial to take glutamine before and during workouts as well. Glutamine is an excellent muscle building supplement which is used to gain muscle as well as preserve muscle when dieting.

Flaxseed or Fish Oil
Flaxseed and fish oil contains omega-3 fatty acids. These fatty acids have numerous health benefits such as preventing heart disease, inflammation, lowers bad cholesterol, prevents clots in arteries, helps recovery, improves liver function and assists in preventing many other diseases. These fats also help the body burn fat.

Multi-vitamins
Intense training depletes your body of nutrients, so they need to be replenished. Chances are you're not going to get the amount of vitamins your body needs in your diet alone, so multi-vitamins are a good way to ensure you're body is getting the essentials.

That's It? Are those the only Supplements that Work?
Not hardly. There are numerous muscle building supplements that work and professionals are finding ways to make supplements more effective by combining certain supplements or ingredients and by more advanced extract processes (the latter is more for herbal supplements). I've personally become a big fan of certain pre workout supplements that contain most of the supplements listed above (the supplements that are essential for pre workout and intra workout) but also pre workout supplements contain some sort of stimulant blend which is often needed for sustainable energy.

Tips on Buying Supplements

- Purchase supplements from reputable supplement companies. There are a lot of superb supplement companies out there that take pride in their products. Is that really true? Well, if you own a supplement company and truly want to deliver supplements that are effective and if you want to stay in business, then yes. If something doesn't work, or if a supplement doesn't product results or if a supplement company shady, the word will spread quickly. The same is true for supplements that work and supplement companies that deliver effective supplements.

- Beware of knock-off supplements. Flip to the back of any bodybuilding or fitness magazine and you'll more than likely see products that have names that mimic the names of certain anabolic steroids or human growth hormone. Not surprisingly most of these so called muscle builders do not list the actual ingredients. The take-home here is don't waste your money.

- Do your own research on muscle building supplements and fat loss supplements. Look at the labels to what's in it then research each ingredient so that you gain a better understanding of how these supplements react in the body. It's a good thing to know what you're putting into your body when taking muscle building supplements.

Universal Nutrition Animal Supplement Stack

One of the supplement brands I've used the most in my years of weight training has been Universal Nutrition supplements. Whereas I do try other brands and types of supplements from time to time I often find myself reverting back to Universal Nutrition supplements. I've always responded well to and have gotten results from Universal and Animal supplements.
This is a very basic supplement stack, like most of my sup plans. As with most of my supplement regimens, I cover here what I feel are essentials along with pre and post workout supplements. I'm also throwing in an extra product from Universal which is a natural testosterone booster.

This **Universal Nutrition** supplement stack is definitely designed for building strength and muscle.

<u>Universal Animal Supplements</u>
1) <u>Animal Pak</u> – daily multi vitamin/training pack
2) <u>Animal Rage</u> – pre workout
3) <u>Universal Atomic 7</u> – BCAAs/glutamine (post workout)
4) <u>Universal Storm</u> – creatine/arginine matrix (post workout)
5) Animal Stak – daily testosterone booster

When taking this supplement stack, I take Animal Pak with my post workout shake. I just took 1 pack a day. Atomic-7 and Storm are my post workout supplements and I took these together in the beginning but later started splitting them up. I started taking Storm immediately after my weight training then I would sip on a serving of Atomic-7 during my cardio which I walk for about 30 minutes.

Universal Nutrition has been around since 1977. They've been widely known as a reputable supplement company and probably have the most hardcore following then any other supplement company.

Animal Pak

It's said that you need to take Animal Pak with some sort of fats (preferably healthy fats) as some of the vitamins are fat soluble so I normally take my AP with my 2nd post workout meal which is usually 3-4 whole eggs and oatmeal. Keep in mind I train early mornings so this is actually my first whole food meal of the day (my first meal is a protein shake, which is immediate post workout; I just prefer to take any multi-vitamins with whole food meals).

If I happen to be taking **Animal Pak** twice a day, which per the label two packs per day is one serving, I'll take my second Animal Pak with my dinner which is a whole food meal. It's rare that I've ever taken Animal Pal twice a day though. On weekends, or non-training days, I'll just take Animal Pak with my breakfast. Anytime of the day is ideal as long as it's taken with food.

My Experience with Animal Pak

Pros: I have more energy in general and just feel better overall. I don't recall ever getting sick while taking Animal Pak either (although I rarely get sick anyway). I like the fact that it contains not only mega doses of essential vitamins and minerals but also the complexes for energy, performance, aminos, antioxidants, and digestive enzymes (I know I just went over this in the last paragraph, but I feel this is a vital point).

Cons: None. I don't really have any complaints about Animal Pak. Some people don't like the fact that there's a ton of pills to swallow and I've heard a few others gripe about the price. Neither of these are issues for me. I'd be concerned if you could jam all of this into 1 tiny little pill and as far as price, you often get what you pay for.

Although I have taken Animal Pak off and on over the years I've started taking it in the beginning of 2011 consistently. In short, no other multi or training pack I've taken compares to Animal Pak, in my opinion. As I stated in the beginning, this type of supplement tends to be last on the list for many (including myself from time to time) and when you run out it doesn't seem to be a huge priority to order another right away. But if you're training hard this should be a priority. I want to also reiterate that you need a quality product, not just any cheap bottle of multi's. Animal Pak isn't just a multi vitamin; there's a butt load of essential ingredients for optimal health and to help you build muscle. In all reality, Animal Pak should be right up there with whey protein in regards to priority.

I must mention that Universal Nutrition has be around since 1977 and still has a hardcore following.

Animal Rage

One of the latest trends in bodybuilding supplements, specifically pre workout supplements, is concentrated (and ultra concentrated) preworkout blends. The idea with concentrated formulas is to take more potent versions of these substances enhancing mental focus, energy, and pumps in the gym. Universal came out with their ultra concentrated Animal Rage in early 2011, a couple years after concentrated blends became popular. Having tried a few concentrated blends I didn't find any substantial difference than what I felt with the regular pre workout formulas I had taken. But I was anxious to try Animal Rage mainly because of Universal's reputation and hardcore following. Plus, much of what I take is Universal and Animal supplements (no, I'm not a rep at the time of writing this but if they ever asked me to be, I'd jump on it).

As with all my reviews I'm not going to go through the label as you can easily find that online. I'm simply going to share my experience with this product. You have 2 options with Rage; you can get it in 44 packs which many Animal products are known for (packs), or you can get the powder which contains 44 servings. From what I've read in forums the powder is the way to go and that's what I bought (so this review is on the powdered version of Animal Rage even though the packs have the same ingredients; I'm guessing the powdered version hits you faster).

My Use/Dosage of Animal Rage

I started out taking 1 scoop of Rage but after a couple of weeks started doing rounded scoops, up to a scoop and a half. I've discussed dosages with a few Animal reps in forums and most of them recommend one scoop. This is a good thing because the 44 servings are a true 44 servings (or at least 30, give or take, in my case) unlike most other pre workout products that say use 2-3 scoops. I only take Rage on my training days, which means I do not take Rage on the weekends (or any pre workout supplement for that matter).

My Experience with Animal Rage

It's important to note that I train early mornings; I wake up around 4:40AM and I'm on my first set by 5AM. That being said, I don't take in a full meal when I wake up but I do need something in my stomach even if it's just a scoop of whey protein. The dilemma is that most pre workout supplements, especially concentrated formulas recommend taking them on an empty stomach. So I would drink my scoop of whey upon waking and about 5 minutes later I'd take Rage. I also tried taking Rage immediately after the scoop of whey and didn't notice any difference. I also don't feel the 1 scoop of whey weakens the affects of Rage (my only explanation for this is that since I'm coming from a 7 hour fast my body is quickly utilizing the whey). I later started taking Rage on its own without the scoop of whey and followed that with aminos acids during my workout (EAA Stack from Universal).

Pros: Animal Rage will definitely get you going and it does grant you the mental focus as well (in other words it's not just a caffeine rush). I don't crash on this stuff either. I get sustainable energy throughout my workout and it seems to 'work' every time I take it. I've taken other pre workout formulas where they'd work for a few days but then had no affect after that. You can't beat the price per serving either.

Cons: If I could change anything about Animal Rage it would be to add an amino acid blend, BCCAs or EAAs, or some sort of whey/casein isolate blend.

I've been taking Animal Rage off and on for a while now. I plan to try Universal's Shock Therapy when I run out of Rage. Will I take Animal Rage again? I'm sure that I will but to be honest I personally like to play around with pre workout supplements, trying new ones as they come out. Part of that reason is because I feel like no matter how great a pre workout product works for you, your body eventually gets used to it and it sort of loses it's effect, or at least the potency, so to speak. That being said I actually like to keep 2 different pre workouts onboard at all times and switch them up every couple of weeks.

However, there are some pre workouts I tend to go back to more than others (and there are many products I'll try and never go back to); I see Rage being one of those I'll go back too often. I've always gotten solid results from most Universal/Animal supplements.

Atomic 7

I haven't tried a ton of BCAA-based supplements though I've had my share of supplements that contain BCAAs as most post workout formulas contain them (if that makes sense). I can attest to a noticeable increase in sustainable energy throughout my workouts when I started taking BCAAs during my workout. With Universal Nutrition Atomic 7 I've noticed a substantial difference in sustainable energy for intra workout. At the time of writing this review, I've been taking Atomic 7 both intra and post workout for almost 2 months now. After that I went 1 day without taking it during my workout just as an experiment and noticed that I 'ran out of gas' a lot earlier in my workout.

My Use/Dosage of Atomic 7

2 scoops per day on workout days (1 scoop = 1 serving). I generally take 1 scoop during my workout and another scoop immediately after my workout.

I take Atomic 7 by itself during my workout, sipping between sets, and (as I'm writing this) I mix 1 scoop of Universal Nutrition Atomic 7 with 1 rounded scoop of Universal Storm and take that post workout (if I were not using Storm I would mix Atomic 7 with another creatine-based supplement, or just plain creatine monohydrate). In the past I've used other post workout formulas and I may go back to that at some point, but for now I'm sticking with Atomic 7 + Storm post workout. On non-training days I usually do not take Atomic 7 at all.

My Experience with Atomic 7

My intent in trying **Atomic 7** was simply for intra workout. I was taking Scivation Xtend before that, which is a great product and I can't really say one is better than the other. I had been taking Universal Storm (a creatine based supplement) for several months because it's very inexpensive and extremely effective; however, I also wanted some sort of amino acid complex to add to my immediate post workout mix, so I started adding a scoop of Atomic 7 to my Storm mix. I've noticed enhanced recovery and have also experienced more muscle fullness wit Atomic 7 added to my supplement regimen. You may be thinking 'why not just buy a post workout formula?' Well, I find Atomic 7 + Storm to not only be just as, if not more effective than any post workout formula I've tried, but also more cost effective.

Pros: The ingredients in Atomic 7 (and the amount of each ingredient) are proven to be effective, the serving size is perfect, and you can't beat the price, of course that's dependent upon where you buy your supplements. More importantly, the bottom line is my workouts are more intense and I have more sustainable energy during my workout. I also feel like I recover faster.

<u>Cons</u>: Nada!

Most of you know I'm a fan of Universal supplements of which many Universal products have become a staple in my supplement plan. I'm a fan of BCAA products as well for intra and post workout. The first product I started taking for intra workout was Scivation Xtend which again is a great product (I believe they now have a new Xtend formula that also includes electrolytes). But what I like more about Universal's Atomic 7 is that it includes taurine, which is known to enhance performance. The bottom line is that using Atomic 7 during and immediately after my workouts has granted me more intense workouts, more sustainable muscle energy, greater recovery, and overall muscle fullness. And I must reiterate that Atomic 7 + Universal Storm is probably the most effective post workout mix I've ever taken.

Uh oh, I didn't rate Atomic 7 for taste! Seriously, I could care less about how a product tastes; what counts is the effectiveness. But I will say I'm pleased with the taste of Atomic 7's flavors so far. I believe I've had what they call 'Way Out Watermelon' and 'Groovy Grape.' They taste fine but again, I'm not taking this stuff for taste. If I want taste, I'll go to a buffet or eat pizza.

Storm

There are a ton of muscle building supplements out there. The thing is most of them really do work to some degree. Some may work better than others, and some people may respond to certain supplements while others may not. One of the most awesome concepts in my opinion regarding supplements is formulas that contain multiple ingredients. Sure, if you're only taking one or two elements it makes sense from a budgeting perspective to go with just a couple stand alone supplements such as creatine or glutamine. The formulas (example: pre and post workout formulas) can be a little pricy. However, I've found one product that's sort of in between meaning that it is comprised of a few solid ingredients but it's also not one of those overpriced products with a long list of ingredients, most of which you don't even know what they are or what they do. That supplement is Storm by Universal Nutrition.

<u>Universal Nutrition Storm – Creatine & Arginine</u>

There are a ton of muscle building supplements out there. The thing is most of them really do work to some degree. Some may work better than others, and some people may respond to certain supplements while others may not. One of the most awesome concepts in my opinion regarding supplements is formulas that contain multiple ingredients. Sure, if you're only taking one or two elements it makes sense from a budgeting perspective to go with just a couple stand alone supplements such as creatine or glutamine. The formulas (example: pre and post workout formulas) can be a little pricy. However, I've found one product that's sort of in between meaning that it is comprised of a few solid ingredients but it's also not one of those overpriced products with a long list of ingredients, most of which you don't even know what they are or what they do. That supplement is Storm by Universal Nutrition.

Basically Universal Nutrition Storm is comprised of two complexes. The first one is called Hypervol Complex which contains 5,000 milligrams of various forms of creatine. In my opinion, creatine is creatine. The different types of creatine you have more to do with absorption. The second complex is called INOXsulin-7. This consists of taurine, betaine anhydrous, citrulline malate, arginine, beta Alanine, ALA and a derivative of leucine. All of this is 3750 milligrams, which isn't very much but probably enough to get the pump effect during a workout. The best part is that this product contains 80 servings and is relatively cheap on most supplement websites. This can be taken before, during and after workouts.

My Use/Dosage of Universal Storm
I've tried Storm several years ago but started it again recently from the time of this review (April 2011). Being hardcore and all, I started taking 2 scoops post workout along with Universal Nutrition's EAA Stack (I feel it's imperative to take amino acids post workout). Well, this sent me to the throne in a bad way for several days. So I stopped taking Storm altogether for a week then jumped back on it only taking 1 rounded scoop post workout. I only take Storm post workout and only take it on training days (no weekends).

*** Late 2011 I started using 1 scoop of Storm with 1 scoop of Universal Atomic 7 post workout.

My Experience with Universal Storm
Pros: At the end of the first week I noticed that I was pumped and my muscles looked a lot fuller than usual. Be careful if you use 2 scoops; as I stated above 2 scoops gave me some major stomach problems but I was fine with 1, and I've found 1 scoop is just as effective. Storm is one of the few bodybuilding supplements that I've gotten noticeable gains from in such a short time. Although I only take Storm post workout you could take this pre and post workout. It's relatively inexpensive too.
Cons: Other than the stomach issues I had with starting out with 2 scoops, I have no complaints here.

Storm is an extremely effective supplement if you're looking for a standard muscle builder. And for the price, you really can't beat it (80 servings and you can usually find Storm for well under $30... that's just crazy compared to what some of the other supplements costs that aren't near as effective). The thing that would make Storm the ultimate post workout supplement is if some BCAAs or EAAs were added.

I always tag the end of any Universal Nutrition product with the fact that Universal has been going strong since 1977.

AminoX

Taken together, these supps will accelerate muscle growth.

hen you want to put the pedal to the metal in your training sessions, you need extra fuel. Including aminos and other crucial nutrients is one of the best ways to accomplish this. To avoid catabolism and to keep your body in an anabolic state, consider adding these supps to your regimen.

▶ BCAAs prevent muscle breakdown and stimulate muscle protein synthesis. Branched-chain amino acids (BCAAs) are a category of three aminos that includes leucine, isoleucine, and valine, and this group is metabolized differently from all the others. BCAAs bypass your liver and are metabolized directly in your muscle tissue, meaning that they more directly fuel the muscle-building process. Two notable benefits are their ability to fuel workouts when they're present before training, and their ability to help you recover from workouts when they're present after training.

▶ Citrulline boosts nitric oxide (NO) levels for better workouts and recovery. Nitric oxide is a molecule that allows your blood vessels to relax so that more blood, oxygen, and nutrients can flow through your system, reaching muscle tissue. One of the most popular ways to increase your NO levels is to supplement with the amino acid arginine that converts to NO. But recent research indicates that taking citrulline, which converts to arginine, may be an even more effective way to increase NO production. Citrulline also helps prevent muscle fatigue while you're training by removing ammonia from your body.

▶ Taurine reduces muscle fatigue and supports muscle cell size. When you weight train, both taurine and strength levels drop as your workout progresses. Supplementing with taurine helps increase muscle endurance as it reduces the oxidative stress that accompanies intense workouts. Taurine helps reduce the levels of lactic acid that accumulate in your muscles as you train, and it allows your muscles to contract more quickly and forcefully, which translates to longer, harder workouts.

▶ Vitamin D supports health and boosts testosterone levels. Recent research has shown a host of benefits that come with vitamin D supplementation: Two of the most important ones for M&F readers include increased strength and higher testosterone. Vitamin D is derived from cholesterol (like testosterone) and it readily converts to a hormone (1,25-dihydroxyvitamin D) that binds to muscle cell membranes, boosting your muscle cells' ability to contract and synthesize protein. Those with vitamin D deficiency often suffer health consequences that include lower testosterone levels. Supplementing with the cholecalciferol form of vitamin D may help overcome this condition.

Get It Together

To maximize muscle building over a specific training phase, you need to give your body what it needs for intense training recovery. BSN's AminoX was formulated with this in mind, and each dose delivers 10 total grams of the aminos on our list and 500 IU of vitamin D. AminoX uses an effervescent delivery system so these nutrients hit your system quickly. take AminoX for a three-to-12-week training phase, then cycle off for four weeks.

Say Yes to Nitric Oxide for the Ultimate Pump

Get your blood flowing and muscles growing with the powerful effects of nitric oxide.

Along with putting in some serious sweat time at the gym, experienced weight trainers understand the importance of supporting their physical efforts with a nutrition and supplement plan that includes a balanced diet, and pre-and post-workout drinks. When these elements are combined with the necessary rest for recovery, the primary pieces are in place for optimal strength and muscle gains.
For many that's enough to satisfy their bodybuilding goals, but what about those looking to further pump up their results? Once you've mastered the exercise and nutrition basics, it's time to look more closely at some other elements that can give you that extra edge in the weight room to take your physique to the next level.

One such element is nitric oxide (N.O.), and when properly used it can payoff big-time. Nitric oxide is a compound made up of nitrogen and oxygen molecules that are produced and used by the body to communicate with other cells. Through the production of amino acids such as L-arginine and L-citrulline, N.O. is naturally present in our bodies.

Nitric Oxide boosters have been among the most popular selling workout supplements due to their effectiveness at widening blood vessels to increase the flow of blood to exercising muscles. This effect is particularly beneficial to weight trainers as increased blood flow means the delivery of more nutrients, oxygen, and anabolic hormones to working muscles. It all adds up to key benefits that will enhance your performance for greater results.

QUICKER RECOVERY

Since an essential factor in a quick recovery is ensuring sufficient nutrients get to the muscle tissues following a strenuous workout, blood flow is of primary significance. By helping to support the amount of blood flow to the tissues, N.O. allows more oxygen delivery to get to the working muscles, which leads to faster recovery times.

INCREASED ENERGY

During a tough workout your body temperature elevates significantly. Without sufficient cooling of the muscle tissues, your body can become overheated. N.O.'s vasodilator effects support the cooling process by improving blood flow to the tissues so less energy will be needed to maintain your body's core temperature - leaving more energy to complete your workouts.

DECREASED FATIGUE

Nothing puts a halt to a good workout session like fatigue. As your exercise intensity ratchets up, your oxygen levels get low. When this happens, lactic acid build-up forming in the muscle tissue takes place, which leads to fatigue, and the likely end of any progress you were making in the weight room. By helping to get more oxygen to the tissues, N.O. is able to reduce the amount of lactic acid build-up and resulting fatigue that goes with it.

BIGGER PUMP

Face it, after you've put in all that hard work at the gym you want to see immediate, visible results. Since the massive muscle pumps you desire are primarily a result of increased blood flow to the muscle tissue, N.O. is the perfect supplement to prime your post-workout muscle pump.

Section 5 : Rest and Recovery

Ultimate Recovery Guide: 6 Keys to Recovery

Being your best doesn't mean just training hard. You need these recovery methods to stay on top of your game.

oo many guys think it's all about the training. Of course, you can't look great unless you consistently train hard, but I would never have been able to achieve the physique I have—and maintained it well into my 40s—if I hadn't listened to my body and given it the best possible chance to fully **recover between workouts**. The six recovery methods I list here are ones that I've found to be completely indispensable. At this point in my life, I consider them just as important as training.

Some of them, like **proper sleep** and stretching, are free. Others, like chiropractic and acupuncture, you need to pay for. All of them are worthwhile investments toward creating the body you want.

All I ask is keep an open mind and be willing to try them. You'll never know what works best for you until you give everything a chance.

6 Keys to Total Recovery

1. SLEEP

You cannot, as many people think, "catch up on" sleep. The body doesn't work that way. You need to get at least eight hours of sleep every night - 10 if you can. Consider it part of your workout, and schedule it just as you would a training session.

. MASSAGE

Lots of guys put off a massage till they're so tight they can barely move. Don't wait that long. Get massages to prevent that in the first place. Go for deep tissue or relaxing massages— or both, to release tension and improve range of motion.

3. CHIROPRACTIC

Heavy lifting over the years put a ton of torque on your joints and spine. But chiropractors can take almost anything that's out of alignment and set it right again. This is a great way to stop serious injuries before they happen.

4. ACUPUNCTURE

This relaxes muscles, relieves stress, and can release toxins. After big heavy-lifting days, I go for an acupuncture session. The whole body comes alive afterward. And check with your insurance provider - many now cover sessions

5. STRETCHING

Don't stretch immediately before you train: Studies show it makes you temporarily weaker. But you still need to maintain flexibility, so do stretch nightly for 20 minutes before bed. And use a foam roller, to break up knots and further release tension.

6. SWIMMING

Low-impact cardio is great, but how about no-impact? Swimming is just that - it gets your heart pounding in no time. It also opens up the body and prevents stiffness by getting all the joints moving through a full range of motion.

How Much Rest is Best?

How much time off do you really need to be your best in the gym? Maybe more than you realize.

You need rest to grow. **Sleep** and time away from the gym are essential to the process of tissue you damage by lifting weights. No matter who you are, there's no way around this fact. But how much rest you need is a question that's dogged exercise scientists for years. Now a new study from Japan suggests that a 12-day deconditioning period, in which no training at all is done, can help resensitize anabolic signals within your muscles-signals that can become desensitized to weight training stimuli over time.

It makes sense: Just as you need two or three vacations a year from work, your body could likely use a vacation from the gym. But is it really necessary to enter a 12-day deconditioning period? And if so, how often?

How Much Time?

According to elite powerlifter and International Sports Sciences Association founder Fred Hatfield, Ph.D., there's no amount of time of that can be prescribed for everyone. "Everybody responds differently to exercise and the lack of exercise," says Hatfield. "It all depends on how hard you train, and the volume and intensity of the eccentric training-that's where the real damage is done. Elite-level powerlifters and bodybuilders could take a week, 10 days, or even longer to fully recover."

Pro bodybuilders, powerlifters, and strongmen (like Derek Poundstone, above) have a preponderance of white muscle fibers-the fibers that trigger high-intensity actions-which are torn to shreds after intense training, necessitating a longer recovery period. But for the average gym rat, a little experimentation is required.

Try a deconditioning period of a week to 10 days after three months of hard training; if you come back to the gym weaker, you rested too long. If so, try waiting up to four months before entering a deconditioning period again, or shorten the period to five to seven days. You'll know you're getting the right amount of rest when you return to the gym and don't feel any weaker. And once you time it just right, your muscles will respond with growth.

Rest Your Body to Grow Your Muscles

Drop the dumbbells and step away from the gym to get better results in the long run.

Question:

Since I rest each body part for 3-4 days before hitting it again, can I weight-train every day?

Answer:

"I'm inclined to say no," says Frank Claps, owner of Fitness For Any Body, a personal-training service in the Lehigh Valley area of Pennsylvania. "Your muscles and the energy systems that fuel them need time to **recover**." In other words, even though individual body parts are getting **rest days**, the overall nervous system, which fuels training for all those body parts, must itself have rest days free from the demands of weight training. If the nervous system doesn't get that rest, it will soon burn out and training will be severely impacted.

Claps points out that many bodybuilders - including professionals - tend to train 4-5 days a week, with a couple of days of rest each week. He agrees with this kind of weekly split. "The best muscle-building results come from having 4-5 days of training with a few rest days within the mix," he explains.

You can also spend some of your non-training days performing moderate cardio and/or **stretching** or other non-gym activities. "Even if your goals are more about health and general fitness than about increased muscle size and strength, training every day is too much," Claps notes. "Without time off from the gym, you won't have the fuel necessary to be at your best and your results will suffer."

Joint Stress

Another factor to take into consideration is the stress that weight training places on joints such as your shoulders, an active joint involved in many upper-body exercises. Even though you may do pushing moves like bench presses on one day and pulling moves like **lat pull downs** the next day, both sessions involve your shoulder, so methodically inserting rest days into your week is sure to help reduce wear and tear.

M&F understands that you love to train, and you want to train as often as possible. While the mere act of going to the gym is an important part of your daily life, you won't get the best results if you go every day, says Claps.

For those who love to train so much that it's hard to skip a day, just apply the same principle to rest and recovery that you apply to training: discipline. Keep yourself from going to the gym one or two days a week, and you'll get better results in the long run.

Deadlift Techniques and Muscle Recovery

workout prescription for improving training performance and results.

"I am recovering from back surgery. What suggestions do you have to lessen the chances of injury when I start deadlifting again?"

After you're cleared by your doctor, you have to start slow. You also need to do some work on finding 'why' you got injured in the first place. Did you get out of position on the last rep? Did you lose your tension when locking the weight out? Was it too much weight or too many reps at that weight? Do you have a weakness that affects your ability to be strong throughout the lift?

Some simple things to think about when you're **deadlifting** are *position* and *tension*.

Basically, can you get into a good position when the bar is on the floor and before you even do the first repetition? Your back should always be straight (neutral), your head should be looking forward or slightly down, and your knees should be as close to the bar as possible. If you can get into this good position, you are more likely to be able to finish in a good position and be safe.

Now, when you get into a good position, the more tension you can create the stronger you'll be (i.e., lift heavier weights) and you'll decrease the likelihood of injury. You can create tension or torque in your shoulders by pulling up on the bar prior to pulling the weight. And creating tension at the hips is done by driving your knees outward against your arms. Remember, the more tension you can create, the stronger you'll be.

Core Strength

Finally, having a stronger core will always help with any compound exercise. A favorite core exercise to improve my deadlift strength is the ab rollout. **Ab rollouts** reinforce a straight back and teach you how to create a large amount of tension across the entire torso. They also strengthen the lats and move the shoulders through a great range of motion, which will help improve your lockout strength.

Doing a little detective work and working on your technique before you start deadlifting again will help you prevent an injury from happening in the future.

"What is the minimum amount of rest my muscles need in order to fully recover?

It really depends on a few really important factors.

What was the intensity of the workout?

Intensity is the key to everything. If you go into the workout and just get through the sets and reps you have written down for the workout, then the session probably wasn't that intense. But if you went in and pushed the pace with the rest periods and lifted the heaviest weight possible for each set - where you couldn't get even one more rep on that last set - then you could probably say the workout was really intense. The more intense the session was, the longer recovery you'll need before your next workout.

What exercises did you use?

Compound exercises not only target more muscle groups and develops serious muscle mass, they are take a toll on the body. Hitting squats, deadlifts, bench presses, pull-ups, and power cleans are more taxing on the body to recover from then tricep kick backs, leg extensions and side laterals.

How good is your recovery?

Are you sleeping 7-9 hours a night? Are you drinking at least half your bodyweight in ounces each day? Are you eating good quality protein, leafy green vegetables and good starches throughout the day? Do you spend enough time **warming up, stretching and hitting mobility work** before and after your workout? The more you focus on recovery, the more often you can train hard and stay mobile. Remember, heavy strength training can make you inflexible and prevent you from moving without restriction. Make your recovery a priority and you'll be able to train hard and remain injury-free.

Think of recovery as a flow that follows a simple wave. After heavy or high intensity training, there must be a period of lower intensity work to ensure you recover to a baseline higher than when you started. This is what training is all about. Training hard, recover, and grow bigger and stronger.

If you train too heavy too long, you will reduce the super-compensation effect associated with working out.

I've heard the numbers 48-72 hours recovery between high intensity training sessions and I've found this to be pretty close to true. If you sleep, and nutrition and hydration

About The Author:

Travis is a graduate of Wichita State University and has Masters Degrees in criminal justice, Physical fitness, Psychology in 4 areas: Sports Psychology Health Psychology Forensic Psychology, Criminal Psychology. He is certified in many specialized computer systems. He is the owner and founder of Digital Overkill, Inc. and specializes in computer forensics, incident response and cybercrimes, often involving work with the largest law firms and corporations nationwide. Travis holds a certificate from the California Department of Justice, Institute of Criminal Investigation as a "Computer Crimes Investigation" specialist. He is also certified as a "Master Instructor" by the California Commission on Peace Officer Standards and Training and is also a licensed National Private Investigator. In addition to his computer forensics and law enforcement work is a certified Defensive Tactics Instructor (DTI) for the Department of Justice, teaching DEA, FBI, Homeland Security and Department of State, and the "sharp edge weapons instructor" , Travis is also a registered dietician, health and fitness instructor, certified strength and conditioning specialist, certified nutritionist, and a certified personal trainer. Travis also earned a Masters in Kinesiology, with an emphasis in exercise and nutrition. His martial arts background is extensive, with a 5th degree black belt in American Kenpo, a 7th degree black belt in Synergy Kenpo, a purple belt in Synergy Brazilian Jiu Jitsu, specifically for the disabled.

Made in United States
Orlando, FL
31 January 2023